# TOEFL® MAP

## MAP Writing

New TOEFL® Edition

### Intermediate

**DARAKWON**

# TOEFL® MAP New TOEFL® Edition
## Writing Intermediate

**Publisher** Chung Kyudo
**Editor** Cho Sangik
**Authors** Jonathan S. McClelland, Shane Spivey
**Designers** Park Narae, Jung Kyuok

First published in November 2022
By Darakwon, Inc.
Darakwon Bldg., 211, Munbal-ro, Paju-si, Gyeonggi-do 10881
Republic of Korea
Tel: 82-2-736-2031 (Ext. 250)
Fax: 82-2-732-2037

**ISBN** 978-89-277-8033-5 14740
978-89-277-8025-0 14740 (set)

**www.darakwon.co.kr**

**Photo Credits**
Shutterstock.com

**Components** Main Book / Scripts and Answer Key
8 7 6 5 4 3 2    24 25 26 27 28

# Introduction

Studying for the TOEFL® iBT is no easy task and is not one that is to be undertaken lightly. It requires a great deal of effort as well as dedication on the part of the student. It is our hope that, by using *TOEFL® Map Writing Intermediate* as either a textbook or a study guide, the task of studying for the TOEFL® iBT will become somewhat easier for the student and less of a burden.

Students who wish to excel on the TOEFL® iBT must attain a solid grasp of the four important skills in the English language: reading, listening, speaking, and writing. The Darakwon *TOEFL® Map* series covers all four of these skills in separate books. There are also three different levels in all four topics. This book, *TOEFL® Map Writing Intermediate*, covers the writing aspect of the test at the intermediate level. Students who want to read passages, listen to lectures, learn vocabulary items, and write essays in response to tasks that appear on the TOEFL® iBT will have their wishes granted by using this book.

*TOEFL® Map Writing Intermediate* has been designed for use in both a classroom setting and as a study guide for individual learners. For this reason, it offers a comprehensive overview of the TOEFL® iBT Writing section. In Part A, the Integrated and Independent Tasks of the TOEFL® iBT Writing section are explained, and writing tips to assist students are included. In Part B, learners have the opportunity to build their background knowledge by studying reading passages, lectures, and writing tasks that have appeared on the TOEFL® iBT. In addition, each chapter includes vocabulary word sections that enable learners to understand the words that frequently appear in the TOEFL® iBT Writing section and incorporate them into their writing. Every chapter also features paraphrasing and summarizing exercises and sample response analysis questions to help learners become more adept at analyzing arguments made in the reading passages and the lectures and creating essays in response. Finally, in Part C, students can take two complete TOEFL® iBT practice tests. Each of these tests includes Integrated and Independent Writing Tasks that have appeared on the actual TOEFL® iBT Writing section. When combined, all of these practice exercises help learners prepare themselves to take and, more importantly, excel on the TOEFL® iBT.

*TOEFL® Map Writing Intermediate* has a vast amount of information and should prove to be invaluable as a study guide for learners who are preparing for the TOEFL® iBT. However, while this book is comprehensive, it is up to each person to do the actual work. In order for *TOEFL® Map Writing Intermediate* to be of any use, the individual learner must dedicate him or herself to studying the information found within its pages. While we have strived to make this book as user friendly and as full of crucial information as possible, ultimately, it is up to each person to make the best of the material in the book. We wish you luck in your study of both English and the TOEFL® iBT, and we hope that you are able to use *TOEFL® Map Writing Intermediate* to improve your skills in both of them.

Jonathan S. McClelland
Shane Spivey

# TABLE OF CONTENTS

## Part C | Experiencing the TOEFL iBT Actual Tests

## Appendix | Master Word List

# How Is This Book Different?

*TOEFL® Map Writing Intermediate* is not a typical TOEFL® study book. Of course, it is similar to other TOEFL® books in that it replicates the types of passages and questions you will come across on the test. However, this book differs in its focus: critical thinking. *TOEFL® Map Writing Intermediate* will teach you how to critically analyze the material you will see on the actual writing section of the TOEFL®, so it will give you the skills needed to earn a top score on the test. Here are the standout features of this book:

## Critical Analysis

### Paraphrasing and Summarizing

To be successful on the writing section of the TOEFL® iBT test, students must be able to paraphrase and summarize information accurately. Therefore, this book includes paraphrase and summary exercises after the reading passage and the lecture.

### Strong Response Analysis

One of the best ways to learn is from examples. It is for this reason that each chapter includes a benchmark sample response after the student writing task. These benchmark responses let you see what makes a response strong and also allow you to deconstruct the answer to understand how it presents the material from the reading passage and the lecture.

### Weak Response Analysis

In addition to the benchmark responses in each chapter, *TOEFL® Map Writing Intermediate* includes a weak response in each chapter for you to analyze. The weak responses allow you to see common errors made by test takers and give you the opportunity to correct theses mistakes. By doing this, you will learn what mistakes you should avoid in your own writing, thus increasing your change for success on the actual TOEFL® iBT.

## Intuitive Integrated Note Taking

### Tandem Note-Taking for Integrated Writing

*TOEFL® Map Writing Intermediate* includes a unique tandem note-taking section. The tandem note-taking section requires you to complete side-by-side outlines for both the reading passage and the lecture. Having notes for both the reading and the lecture next to each other on the same page will allow you to analyze the relationship between them more quickly, easily, and accurately.

### Idea Boxes for Independent Writing

For many students, generating supporting ideas is the most difficult aspect of the Independent Writing Task. Therefore, this book includes idea boxes with questions that will help you generate supporting ideas and examples for your essay.

## Vocabulary Building

### Vocabulary Boxes

To earn a high score on the TOEFL® iBT, a strong vocabulary is essential. For this reason, each chapter in *TOEFL® Map Writing Intermediate* includes two vocabulary boxes in the Integrated Writing Section. Each vocabulary box includes six to ten words and gives the part of speech, the definition, and the use in context for each word. This will enable you to identify these words successfully when they appear on the actual TOEFL® iBT while allowing you to make your writing more vivid and succinct.

# How to Use
# This Book

*TOEFL® Map Writing Intermediate* is designed for use either as a textbook in a classroom or in a TOEFL® iBT preparation course or as a study guide for individuals who are studying for the TOEFL® iBT on their own. *TOEFL® Map Writing Intermediate* has been divided into three sections: Part A, Part B, and Part C. All three sections offer information that is important to learners preparing for the TOEFL® iBT. Part A is divided into 3 chapters that introduce the Writing section, the Integrated Writing Task, and the Independent Writing Task. Part B is divided into 8 chapters, and each chapter includes passages and questions similar to those that have appeared on the TOEFL® iBT. Part C has 2 actual tests consisting of Integrated and Independent Writing Tasks that resemble those appearing on the TOEFL® iBT.

## Part A  Understanding Writing Question Types

This section is designed to acquaint learners with the TOEFL® iBT Writing section and is divided into 3 chapters. The first chapter provides an overview of the Writing section and explains the general requirements of the Integrated and Independent Writing Tasks. It also features an explanation of how to organize essays and includes an exercise for learners to complete. The second chapter breaks down the Integrated Writing Task by providing a detailed explanation of the question types and the writing requirements and includes a sample Integrated Writing reading passage, lecture, and question. This chapter also provides writing tips, explains the note-taking and sample response sections included throughout the book, and has learner exercises for both chapters. The final chapter breaks down the Independent Writing Task by providing a detailed explanation of the question types and the writing requirements for this task. This chapter includes writing tips, emphasizes developing organizational skills when writing, and includes a sample Independent Writing Task question.

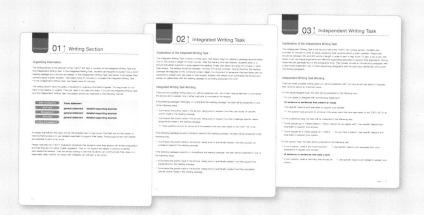

# Part B  Building Knowledge & Skills for the Writing Test

The purpose of this section is to introduce passages on various topics that have appeared on the TOEFL® iBT. There are 8 chapters in Part B. Each one includes an Integrated Writing Task and an Independent Writing Task as well as vocabulary boxes and paraphrasing, summarizing, and sample response analysis exercises. Each chapter is divided into several parts.

## Integrated Writing Task – Reading Passage

This section begins by introducing 6 to 10 new vocabulary words that appear in the reading passage. Following the reading passage are paraphrasing and summarizing exercises designed to help students fully understand the reading passage and explain it in their own words.

## Integrated Writing Task – Lecture

This section is similar to the reading passage section. It introduces 6 to 10 new vocabulary words that are included in the lecture. Also like the reading passage section, this section contains paraphrasing and summarizing exercises designed to help students understand the lecture and explain it in their own words. This will enable them to write a higher-scoring response for the writing task.

## Integrated Writing Task – Tandem Note-Taking

This section requires students to briefly summarize the information from the previous two sections in two vertical columns. This arrangement allows students to expand their notes by adding supporting details from the reading passage and lecture while allowing them to better understand the relationship between the two passages.

## Integrated Writing Task – Writing Section and Scaffolding

This section includes the question for the Integrated Writing Task and provides space for students to write their responses. It also features a writing guide to help students organize their essays as they write. At the end of this section is the scaffolding portion, which includes useful phrases for students to incorporate into their responses.

## Integrated Writing Task – Strong Response

This section features a well-written response to the writing task given in the previous section. Students can see how to improve their own responses by analyzing the organizational techniques, the transitions, and the vocabulary used in the strong response.

## Integrated Writing Task – Weak Response

This section features a weak response that scores between a 1 and 4 on Integrated Writing Scoring Rubric. Students can see common mistakes to avoid in their own responses. At the end of this section is a critical-thinking exercise that allows students to further analyze the potential strengths and weaknesses of the response.

## Independent Writing Task – Generating Ideas

This section begins by presenting the Independent Writing Task question for the chapter. This is followed by an idea-generating exercise that assists students in developing supporting ideas for their responses.

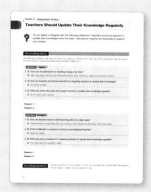

## Independent Writing Task – Planning

This section consists of a detailed outlining exercise that requires students to write their thesis statement, supporting ideas, and examples.

## Independent Writing Task – Writing Section and Scaffolding

This section reintroduces the writing task for the chapter and provides space for students to write their responses. It also features a writing guide to help students organize their essays as they write. At the end of this section is the scaffolding portion, which includes useful phrases for learners to incorporate into their essays.

## Independent Writing Task – Strong Response

This section features a well-written response to the writing task given in the previous section. Students can see how to improve their own responses by analyzing the organization, the transitions, the main ideas, and the examples used in the strong response.

## Independent Writing Task – Weak Response

This section features a weak response that scores between a 1 and 4 on Independent Writing Scoring Rubric. Students can see common mistakes to avoid in their own responses. At the end of this section is a critical-thinking exercise that allows students to further analyze the potential strengths and weaknesses of the response.

# Part C Experiencing the TOEFL iBT Actual Tests

This section contains 2 complete TOEFL® iBT Writing section tests. The purpose of this section is to let students experience the actual Writing section and to see if they can apply the skills they have learned in the course of studying *TOEFL® Map Writing Intermediate*.

# Part **A**

# Understanding Writing Question Types

**01** Writing Section

## Organizing Information

The writing section is the last part of the TOEFL® iBT test. It consists of the Integrated Writing Task and the Independent Writing Task. In the Integrated Writing Task, students are required to explain how a short reading passage and a lecture are related. In the Independent Writing Task, test takers must explain their opinions about a given situation. Test takers have 20 minutes to complete the Integrated Writing Task. For the Independent Writing Task, test takers have 30 minutes.

The writing section tests the ability of students to organize information logically. The responses do not have to be creative or original. They just need to be clear and direct. For both the Integrated Writing Task and the Independent Writing Task, the essays should be organized in the following manner:

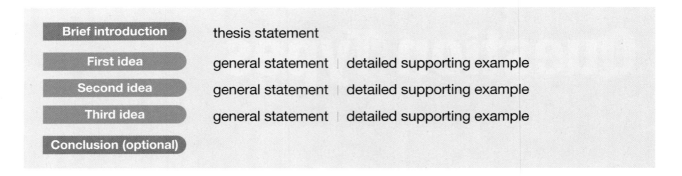

| Brief introduction | thesis statement | |
| First idea | general statement | detailed supporting example |
| Second idea | general statement | detailed supporting example |
| Third idea | general statement | detailed supporting example |
| Conclusion (optional) | | |

An essay that follows this basic format will probably earn a high score. The best way for test takers to improve their scores is to use detailed examples to support their ideas. Strong support and vivid details are essential to earn a top score.

Please note that the TOEFL® evaluators recognize that students write their essays with limited preparation and that they are not native English speakers. They do not expect test takers to produce polished, well-researched essays. They are simply looking to see that students can communicate their ideas in a reasonably clear manner. An essay with mistakes can still earn a top score.

# Information Organization Exercise

Each of the following boxes contains ideas for an essay. Organize the information so that it fits logically into the outlines provided below.

**1**
- Playing competitive sports can stress children out.
- Children who play competitive sports are usually more violent.
- Children are more sensitive than adults.
- Children just want to have fun with their friends.

- Playing to win can make children too aggressive.
- Most children do not care about winning or losing.
- Children should only play sports for fun.

- ■ **Thesis Statement**

- ■ **First Supporting Argument**

  Detailed Supporting Example

- ■ **Second Supporting Argument**

  Detailed Supporting Example

- ■ **Third Supporting Argument**

  Detailed Supporting Example

**2**
- Speaking a second language can help you get a job.
- Understanding a foreign language makes it easier to communicate with more people.
- Knowing a second language shows employers that you are hard working.
- Studying a foreign language also makes you smarter.

- Learning another language has many benefits.
- By learning Spanish, you can communicate with 570 million people.
- It helps develop the parts of the brain related to speech.

- ■ **Thesis Statement**

- ■ **First Supporting Argument**

  Detailed Supporting Example

- ■ **Second Supporting Argument**

  Detailed Supporting Example

- ■ **Third Supporting Argument**

  Detailed Supporting Example

## Explanation of the Integrated Writing Task

The Integrated Writing Task consists of three parts. Test takers begin by reading a passage approximately 230 to 300 words in length for three minutes. After the reading time has finished, students listen to a lecture that either supports or goes against the reading. Finally, test takers are given 20 minutes to write their essays. The essays should be between 150 and 225 words in length. During this time, the reading passage will reappear on the computer screen. Again, it is important to remember that test takers are not expected to present any new ideas in their essays. Instead, test takers must summarize the lecture and explain its relationship with the reading passage by providing examples from both.

## Integrated Writing Task Wording

There are five possible writing tasks you will be presented with. All of them require learners to summarize the lecture and to explain how it either supports or contradicts the reading.

If the listening passage challenges or contradicts the reading passage, the task will be presented in one of the following ways:

→ Summarize the points made in the lecture, being sure to explain how they cast doubt on specific points made in the reading passage.

→ Summarize the points made in the lecture, being sure to explain how they challenge specific claims [arguments] made in the reading passage.

**cf.** *These questions account for almost all of the questions that have been asked on the TOEFL® iBT so far.*

If the listening passage answers problems raised in the reading passage, the task will be presented in the following way:

→ Summarize the points made in the lecture, being sure to specifically explain how they answer the problems raised in the reading passage.

If the listening passage supports or strengthens the reading passage, the task will be presented in one of the following ways:

→ Summarize the points made in the lecture, being sure to specifically explain how they support the explanations in the reading passage.

→ Summarize the points made in the lecture, being sure to specifically explain how they strengthen specific points made in the reading passage.

# Writing Tips for the Integrated Writing Task

◆ Take notes on all of the main ideas from the reading passage and the lecture. The notes do not have to be complete, but they should include the supporting arguments and the examples for each idea from both the reading passage and the lecture.

◆ Write your notes in two columns with the notes for the reading passage on the left and the notes for the lecture on the right. This will make it easier for you to compare their main ideas when it is time for you to write.

◆ Take one minute to organize your ideas before you begin writing. Refer to your notes as you write.

◆ Focus primarily on summarizing the lecture in your response. Be sure to include all of the main ideas and examples from the lecture. Do not give your opinion about the topic.

◆ Use only one or two sentences per paragraph to explain how the reading relates to the lecture.

◆ Keep the same format throughout your essay. You can begin each body paragraph by summarizing the reading passage and then explain how it relates to the lecture. Or you can do the opposite by starting with the lecture and explaining how it relates to the reading passage.

◆ Begin each paragraph with clear, simple transitions.

◆ Manage your time wisely. Try to spend no more than five minutes writing each paragraph.

◆ Use the last one to three minutes to proofread your response. Correct errors as needed.

# Sample Integrated Writing Task

## ✪ Reading Passage

On the Integrated Writing Task, a reading passage like the one below will be given to you first. You will have three minutes to read the passage.

With the growing threat of world hunger, people are looking for new ways to end this crisis. One of these is through the use of genetically modified organisms, otherwise known as GMOs. These plants are specially created by scientists to be superior to traditional crops. This makes genetically modified foods the best tool for fighting world hunger.

One benefit of GMOs is their resistance to insect pests. Each year, farmers around the world use millions of tons of insecticides to stop bugs from eating their crops. These insect killers are made from powerful chemicals that can harm the surrounding environment as well as the crops themselves. With GMOs, farmers no longer have to rely on insecticides. This protects the environment and makes foods safer to eat.

Another advantage of modified foods is their increased crop yield. Traditional crops produce a relatively small amount of food per acre. For instance, one acre of corn produces about 120 bushels each year. With GMOs, farmers can produce much more food with the same amount of land. One acre of genetically modified corn can produce nearly 200 bushels per year. It is for this reason that poor farmers with limited land resources rely on GMOs to help them grow enough food to survive.

Perhaps the most important aspect of GMOs is their greater nutritional value. Vitamins and minerals can easily be added to genetically modified foods to help people stay healthy. The best-known example of this is GM rice, commonly referred to as golden rice. Golden rice was created to help the millions of people in developing nations who do not get enough vitamin A in their diets. Thanks to golden rice and other GMOs, millions of people each year are able to get the nutrients they need to stay healthy.

Following this, you will listen to a lecture:

## ✪ Lecture

### Narrator (Male)

Now listen to part of a lecture on the topic you just read about.

01-01

### Professor (Male)

In many ways, technology has made our lives safer, cleaner, and more enjoyable. There are some areas, though, where the use of technology is not such a good thing. One of these areas is food. Specifically, I'm referring to genetically modified crops, or GMOs. These artificially created crops pose a serious risk to both people and the environment.

First of all, growing genetically modified crops can damage the environment. How does this occur? Pollen from modified crops can reach other areas. This spreads the genes from GMOs to unmodified plant species. So these natural plants develop the traits of GMOs. One trait is resistance to herbicides . . . you know, weed killers. This has caused the appearance of so-called superweeds that cannot be killed with herbicides. As a result, many farmers have been forced to switch back to growing traditional crops.

And do you know what else? GMO crops and farming technology are expensive, meaning that farmers in poorer nations cannot afford them. Although genetically modified crops were created to help these people, only farmers in rich nations can easily afford to grow these crops. The truth of the matter is that fewer than ten percent of farmers in developing nations grow GM crops. This makes it difficult for poor farmers to reap the benefits of their increased food production.

Oh, and here's another concern with GMOs: food safety. You know, natural foods have developed over a long period of time, so our bodies are used to them. But with GM foods, this is not the case. In fact, these foods may create problems such as introducing new allergens into foods and contributing to the spread of antibiotic resistance. It is for this reason that most nations around the world have banned the production and importation of GM foods.

Once the listening is finished, the reading passage will reappear along with the following directions and the writing task:

## ✪ Directions and Writing Task

**Directions** You have 20 minutes to plan and write your response. Your response will be judged on the basis of the quality of your writing and on how well your response presents the points in the lecture and their relationship to the passage. Typically, an effective response will be 150-225 words.

**Question** Summarize the points made in the lecture, being sure to explain how they cast doubt on specific points made in the reading passage.

At this time, you will have 20 minutes to complete your essay.

# Paraphrasing and Summarizing

To be successful on the writing portion of the TOEFL®, you must be able to paraphrase sentences by rewriting them in your own words and by summarizing the information. The following exercises show you how to do this successfully.

## ⊘ Sample Paraphrasing

The following sentences from the reading passage can be paraphrased in the following ways.

---

1  These plants are specially created by scientists to be superior to traditional crops.

⋯▸ *Scientists have produced GM crops to improve upon natural crops.*

2  These insect killers are made from powerful chemicals that can harm the surrounding environment as well as the crops themselves.

⋯▸ *Both the environment and crops can be damaged by the chemicals found in insecticides.*

3  With GMOs, farmers can produce much more food with the same amount of land.

⋯▸ *GM crops allow farmers to grow more food without having to use more land.*

4  Golden rice was created to help the millions of people in developing nations who do not get enough vitamin A in their diets.

⋯▸ *To help poor people get the nutrition they need, scientists created genetically modified rice.*

---

## ⊘ Sample Summarizing

The summary below consists of paraphrased information from the reading passage.

---

The author of the reading passage argues that genetically modified foods are the solution for the world's hunger crisis. Three arguments are given to support this idea. The first is that GM foods cannot be damaged by insects, meaning that they do not need insecticides. This, in turn, benefits the environment. Second, the author contends that these crops can help poor farmers because they produce more food per acre than traditional crops. The last point is that GMOs have greater nutritional value. This, it is argued, makes it possible for people in developing nations to get the nutrients they need to stay healthy.

---

As you can see, the paraphrased sentences convey the ideas of the original sentences with different words while the summary clearly explains the main idea of the reading passage and its supporting details.

# ✪ Sample Paraphrasing and Summarizing Exercise

You will now listen to the lecture. As you listen, complete the paraphrasing and summarizing exercises below. Try to make your answers similar to the ones given for the reading passage.

---

**Paraphrasing Exercise**

1   These artificially created crops pose a serious risk to both people and the environment.

   ⋯▸ *Both humans and* _____ *can be* _____ *by GM crops.*

2   Pollen from modified crops can reach other areas, spreading the genes from GMOs to unmodified plant species.

   ⋯▸ *GM crops can* _____ *to other plants by fertilizing them*

   _____ .

3   Although genetically modified crops were created to help these people, only farmers in rich nations can easily afford to grow these crops.

   ⋯▸ *Only* _____ *can purchase GM crops even though they were made*

   _____ .

4   It is for this reason that most nations around the world have banned the production and importation of GM foods.

   ⋯▸ *Numerous countries* _____ *the growth and sale of* _____

   *for safety reasons.*

---

**Summarizing Exercise**

In the lecture, the professor questions _____ as a means to solve world hunger.
His first argument explains how GM crops can _____ by spreading their traits to
other plant species. His next point is about the high costs of GMO farming technology. Even though
these crops were developed to help poor farmers, they are _____ for these
people to purchase. This negates the benefits of increased crop production of GMOs. The instructor
concludes his lecture by _____ of GM crops. He explains that because they
cause _____ , these crops have been banned in numerous countries.

## Tandem Note-Taking

Now it is time for you to complete the chart below by using the information from the paraphrasing and summarizing exercises for the reading and listening. These notes will help you when you write your response.

<table>
<tr><td>READING</td><td>LISTENING</td></tr>
<tr><td>

**Main Idea**

*GMOs are the best solution for ending world hunger.*

**First Supporting Argument**

*GM foods are resistant to*

Supporting Detail

**Second Supporting Argument**

*These crops produce more*

Supporting Detail

**Third Supporting Argument**

*GMOs can help end*

Supporting Detail

</td><td>

**Main Idea**

*GM crops pose a risk to both people and the environment.*

**First Supporting Argument**

*GMOs can cause damage to*

Supporting Detail

**Second Supporting Argument**

*GMO crops and technology are*

Supporting Detail

**Third Supporting Argument**

*Scientists are still not sure of*

Supporting Detail

</td></tr>
</table>

# Writing Exercise

Use this page to write your response. You have 20 minutes to complete your essay.

Part A | 21

## Writing Guide

Summarize the points made in the lecture, being sure to explain how they cast doubt on specific points made in the reading passage.

**First Paragraph** ○

State and discuss thesis

**Second Paragraph** ○

First main idea from lecture

Supporting detail

Contradiction from reading

**Third Paragraph** ○

Second main idea from lecture

Supporting detail

Contradiction from reading

**Fourth Paragraph** ○

Third main idea from lecture

Supporting detail

Contradiction from reading

**Fifth Paragraph** ○

Conclusion (optional)

# Strong Response

Read the response carefully to see what makes a response strong. Place the following titles in the appropriate blanks in the response.

a. Contradictory sentence (×3)   b. Topic sentence (×3)   c. Thesis statement

d. Opening sentence   e. Example (×3)

[    ] The author of the reading passage argues in favor of using genetically modified foods to help solve world hunger. [    ] The lecturer, on the other hand, does not agree with this viewpoint.

[    ] The reading passage first explains that GMOs are not vulnerable to insect pests and therefore do not require insecticides. [    ] Meanwhile, the professor contends that genetically modified crops can harm the environment by spreading their traits to other plants. [    ] He illustrates this point by explaining that this process has resulted in superweeds that cannot be killed by herbicides, which has forced farmers to go back to traditional crops.

[    ] Next, the reading passage states that GM crops produce more food per acre than regular crops. [    ] This argument is countered by the instructor. [    ] He posits that because GMO crops and technology are so expensive, farmers from developing nations cannot afford them. This, the professor believes, offsets the benefits of increased crop production from GMOs.

[    ] The last point made by the reading passage is that GM foods are healthier than traditional foods. [    ] The example given is golden rice, which contains high amounts of vitamin A. [    ] The lecturer, on the other hand, questions the safety of GMOs. He believes that they introduce new allergens into foods and add to the spread of antibiotic resistance. This is why many nations have banned the growth and sale of genetically modified foods.

# Weak Response

Read the response carefully and make note of any errors in grammar and logic.

> The professor and the reading have different opinions about GMO foods. The professor is against them, but the reading is favor of them.
>
> In the beginning, the professor says that GMO unable to resist weed killers. He also say that some weeds cannot be kill by killers. So this is a problem. The reading was the opposite. It said that GMO create better environment. This is because they don't use insects. So in this way they better.
>
> Secondly the professor talks that GMO are too expensive for poor farmers to have. They can not grow them. Only rich farmers can afford them. Therefore, this is a problem. In the passage, it was contrast. It wrote the GMO save farmers who are poor.
>
> Third, the professor believe that GMO are unhealthy. **1** Therefore, they are not allowed in many country. **2** But the reading passage stated opposite again. **3** It said GMO have fixed world hunger, such as gold rice. This has given poor people vitamin a.

## ✪ Analysis Exercise

1 In which of the following ways should the highlighted sentence be rewritten?

   Ⓐ Farmers who use GM crops must be poor, according to the argument in the reading.

   Ⓑ The passage states that poor farmers can use GM crops to help them survive.

   Ⓒ The points made by the author differ from those made in the reading.

2 Where should the following sentence be added to improve the response?

**GM crops may contribute to the spread of antibiotic resistance and introduce new allergens into foods.**

   Ⓐ **1**

   Ⓑ **2**

   Ⓒ **3**

# Integrated Writing Scoring Rubric

The scoring rubric below is similar to the one used by the TOEFL® iBT Writing Task graders.

## Score 5

A response scoring a 5 clearly summarizes the central ideas from the lecture and explains how they relate to the arguments given in the reading passage. Essays of this level are well organized and contain very few grammatical errors that do not obscure meaning.

## Score 4

A response scoring at this level is generally successful at presenting the main ideas from the lecture and explaining how they relate to those presented in the reading passage. However, it may occasionally be unclear or inaccurate. A response will also earn a score of 4 if it includes more frequent and noticeable grammatical errors that only occasionally obscure meaning.

## Score 3

A response scoring at this level generally explains the main ideas from the lecture and how they relate to those presented in the reading passage but does so in a way that is vague, unclear, or occasionally incorrect. A response that fails to include one of the main ideas from the lecture will also score at this level. Finally, essays of this level may contain more frequent grammatical errors that make it difficult to understand the relationship between the arguments made in the lecture and reading passage.

## Score 2

A response scoring at this level includes only some of the important ideas from the lecture and fails to explain how they relate to the information presented in the reading passage. A response scoring a 2 may also include serious grammatical errors that prevent readers who are not already familiar with the topic from understanding the main ideas from the lecture and reading passage.

## Score 1

A response scoring at this level includes little or no useful information from the lecture. It may also include very low-level language that completely obscures understanding.

## Score 0

A response scoring at this level simply copies sentences from the reading, does not address the topic, is written in a foreign language, or is blank.

# 03 Independent Writing Task

## Explanation of the Independent Writing Task

The Independent Writing Task is the second half of the TOEFL® iBT writing section. Students are provided 30 minutes to write an essay explaining their opinions about a given question. Responses should be between 300 and 400 words in length in order to earn a high score. To earn a top score, test takers must use logical arguments and effective supporting examples to support their arguments. Strong responses are generally four or five paragraphs long. They usually include an introductory paragraph with a clear thesis statement, two or three supporting paragraphs with focused topic sentences, and a brief concluding paragraph.

## Independent Writing Task Wording

There are three possible writing tasks you will be presented with, but they all ask test takers to express their opinions about an important issue.

For the agree/disagree type, the task will be presented in the following way:

→ Do you agree or disagree with the following statement?

**[A sentence or sentences that present an issue]**

Use specific reasons and examples to support your answer.

cf. *This question type accounts for almost all of the essay topics that have been asked on the TOEFL® iBT so far.*

For the preference type, the task will be presented in the following way:

→ Some people say X. Others believe Y. Which opinion do you agree with? Use specific reasons and examples to support your answer.

→ Some people do X. Other people do Y. Which . . . do you think is better? Use specific reasons and examples to support your opinion.

For the opinion type, the task will be presented in the following way:

→ In your opinion, what is the most important . . . ? Use specific reasons and examples from your experience to explain your answer.

→ **[A sentence or sentences that state a fact]**

In your opinion, what is one thing that should be . . . ? Use specific reasons and details to explain your choice.

## Writing Tips for the Independent Writing Task

◆ Spend three to five minutes brainstorming and outlining your response before you begin writing.

◆ Rewrite the question in your thesis statement.

◆ Make a few general statements about the topic in your opening paragraph.

◆ Include at least two main ideas in your essay to support your opinion.

◆ Give supporting ideas and examples from your personal experience and knowledge to strengthen your response.

◆ Conclude each body paragraph with a sentence summarizing its main argument.

◆ Manage your time wisely. Try not to spend more than seven to ten minutes writing each paragraph.

◆ Use the last one to three minutes to proofread your response. Correct errors as needed.

## Sample Independent Writing Task

On the Independent Writing Task, you will be given the following directions along with a similar writing prompt:

**Directions** Read the question below. You have 30 minutes to plan, write, and revise your essay. Typically, an effective response will contain a minimum of 300 words.

**Question** Do you agree or disagree with the following statement?

**It was easier to be successful in the past than it is today.**

Use specific reasons and examples to support your answer.

# Generating Ideas

The following questions will help you write your response. Answer each with one or two sentences. Plan an answer for both options. Some ideas have been provided to help you.

**Idea Box** **Agree**

**1 Q** In what ways was there less competition in the past in terms of education?

**A** *In the past, very few people were well educated or attended college.*

**2 Q** How has the number of skills a person needs changed over time?

**A** *People today need*

**3 Q** How has the definition of success changed over time?

**A** *It has become*

Reason 1:

Reason 2:

Reason 3:

**Idea Box** **Disagree**

**1 Q** What was the work ethic of most people like in the past?

**A** *At that time, many people worked long hours at difficult jobs. Few people had easy jobs.*

**2 Q** What opportunities did most people have to become successful?

**A** *Most people had*

**3 Q** What types of people were usually the most successful in the past?

**A** *At that time, the most successful people*

Reason 1:

Reason 2:

Reason 3:

# Outlining Exercise

To be successful on the writing portion of the TOEFL®, you must get into the habit of outlining your essay before you begin writing. Start by writing your thesis statement and then arrange your supporting ideas logically. Finally, write down at least one supporting example for each supporting idea.

## ✪ Planning

Use the outline to plan your response to the following: Do you agree or disagree with the following statement? It was easier to be successful in the past than it is today. Use specific reasons and examples to support your answer.

| Agree | Disagree |
|---|---|
| **Thesis Statement** | **Thesis Statement** |
| *I wholeheartedly agree that it was easier to be successful in the past.* | *I believe that it is easier to be successful today than it was in times before.* |
| **First Supporting Idea** | **First Supporting Idea** |
| Supporting Example | Supporting Example |
| **Second Supporting Idea** | **Second Supporting Idea** |
| Supporting Example | Supporting Example |
| **Third Supporting Idea** | **Third Supporting Idea** |
| Supporting Example | Supporting Example |
| **Conclusion (optional)** | **Conclusion (optional)** |

# Writing Exercise

Use this page to write your response. You have 30 minutes to complete your essay.

## Writing Guide

Do you agree or disagree with the following statement? It was easier to be successful in the past than it is today. Use specific reasons and examples to support your answer.

**First Paragraph**

State and discuss thesis

**Second Paragraph**

First main supporting idea

General statement

Supporting example

**Third Paragraph**

Second main supporting idea

General statement

Supporting example

**Fourth Paragraph**

Third main supporting idea

General statement

Supporting example

**Fifth Paragraph**

Conclusion

## Strong Response

Read the response carefully to see what makes a response strong. Place the following titles in the appropriate blanks in the response.

| a. Summary | b. Opening sentences | c. General statement (×3) | d. Thesis statement |
| e. Example (×3) | f. Topic sentence (×3) | g. Final comment | |

[    ] I disagree that it was easier to be successful in the past than it is today for three reasons. [    ] First, in previous times working hard was necessary just to get by. Second, there were fewer opportunities for average people to excel. Finally, the people who were successful in the past were highly gifted and diligent.

[    ] To begin with, most people in the past needed to work hard in order to survive. [    ] They worked long hours at difficult jobs. [    ] To be more specific, it was common to work sixty hours or more per week at physically difficult jobs. Therefore, people had little time or energy to do more than what was required of them. Today, many people work in office jobs for only forty hours per week. Because they have more free time and energy, they are able to do extra work to get ahead. In this way, it is easier for employees today to stand out.

[    ] Another factor that made it difficult to be successful in the past was that there were fewer opportunities for people to get ahead. [    ] For centuries, the vast majority of people learned a trade from a young age or worked on their families' farms. They could not easily do something different or unique. [    ] This is illustrated by the fact that most successful people in the past were born into royal or rich families. These privileged members of society received the best educations and had many opportunities to succeed. In contrast, unlike today, the majority of average people did not have these opportunities given to them.

[    ] On top of this, middle-class people who were successful in the past were very gifted. [    ] Back then, only people with natural talent could stand out from the common people. [    ] For example, consider the case of Ludwig van Beethoven. His musical ability was evident from an early age, and he was able to develop his skill on his own. If he had not been born with his talent, he might have never become successful. Today, however, average people can compensate for their lack of natural ability by going to college and gaining certification.

[    ] Ultimately, I contend that it is easier for more people to be successful today. [    ] Thanks to increased wealth and educational opportunities, average people can now excel beyond the norm and achieve success.

# Weak Response

Read the response carefully and make note of any errors in grammar and logic.

People today concentrating on success a lot. Many people want to become more rich and famous. That's why its so hard to be successful today because a lot people feel the same way, too. Thus I agree with the statement above.

One reason why it's easier to be successful in the past than today was there was not as many compitition. For example, most people just worked at there jobs. They didn't not go to college. So people were less educate. This means it was possible for average people to become successful easily.

Second reason why it's easier to be successful in the past is not as many skill needed back at that time. Be good at your job didn't mean too much thinking. If you work on the farm, you only need to know about plant crops and grow food. You don't need to use the computer or whatever. Unlike then, today is not true. Now you have to know many things to be successful. You have to know about your job, your computer programs, etc. So therefore less skills needed back in the past.

The final reason I feel this way is people in the past they didn't not care about be successful. They only wanted to have a house and family. They wanted to eat food every night. They did not want the luxury item. This made it successful easily. But today it cannot become successful without lots of money. For example, Bill Gates is successful, but maybe my neighbor isn't not because he is not so rich.

In conclusion, to be successful today is harder than in the past.

## ✪ Analysis Exercise

Q Which of the following sentences could be added to strengthen the response?

- Ⓐ There are a much wider variety of jobs available today compared to previous times.
- Ⓑ In previous times, people who owned their own land were considered successful.
- Ⓒ Simply by graduating from college, a person in the past could become successful easily.

# Independent Writing Scoring Rubric

The scoring rubric below is similar to the one used by the TOEFL® iBT Writing Task graders.

### Score 5

An essay that earns a 5 clearly addresses the topic. It uses logical organization, appropriate transitions between ideas and paragraphs, and developed supporting examples for each main idea. The essay will read smoothly and include a variety of sentence types, suitable word choice, and correct use of idiomatic expressions. It may also include minor grammatical errors that do not distract the reader.

### Score 4

An essay scoring at this level does a good job of addressing the topic. However, it may not include enough details to fully develop its supporting ideas. It is clearly organized for the most part though it may have some unclear transitions, redundancies, and/or unrelated information. It may also include more noticeable errors in grammar and word choice that do not obscure meaning.

### Score 3

An essay that earns a 3 addresses the topic using explanations and examples that are not easily understood or fully developed. Although the response will be somewhat coherent, it may not have clear transitions between ideas. An essay scoring at this level may also include accurate but limited sentence structures and vocabulary and more frequent grammatical errors that occasionally obscure meaning.

### Score 2

An essay scoring at this level fails to address the topic clearly and is characterized by inadequate organization and insufficiently developed ideas. It may include examples that fail to develop the main ideas and more numerous grammatical errors that obscure meaning.

### Score 1

An essay scoring at this level fails to present and develop any ideas and includes serious and frequent grammatical errors that largely obscure meaning.

### Score 0

A response scoring at this level simply copies the topic, does not address the topic, is written in a foreign language, or is blank.

# Building Knowledge & Skills for the Writing Test

# Zoology: **Bonobos and Chimpanzees**

**🔊 Vocabulary**  Take a few moments to review the vocabulary items that will appear in this task.

**genetic** *adj.* relating to the science of heredity, which is the study of how parents pass their characteristics on to their children
DNA and RNA are your body's **genetic** material.

**ancestor** *n.* a forefather; a person coming early in a family line
My **ancestors** were farmers from Europe.

**captivity** *n.* the act of keeping animals
Animals in zoos are being held in **captivity**.

**aggressively** *adv.* forcefully; hostilely; in a hostile manner
The male lions acted **aggressively** toward each other.

**harmony** *n.* social agreement
Human beings should live in **harmony** with nature.

**intense** *adj.* extreme in degree, strength, or size
The heat in the middle of the desert is too **intense** for most people to handle.

**resort to** *phr v.* to look to when in need
The government **resorted to** raising taxes to end the financial problems.

**resolve** *v.* to find a solution to a problem or argument
After many weeks of fighting, my brother and I were able to **resolve** our argument.

## Reading

Read the passage carefully. Try to understand what the main argument of the passage is. You have 3 minutes to read.

Bonobos and chimpanzees are two of humans' closest genetic relatives. Because these animals share a common ancestor, bonobos and chimpanzees have many characteristics in common. However, they are also unique in many ways. One of the biggest differences between the animals is their attitudes. While bonobos tend to be peaceful, chimpanzees are often more violent.

Observations of bonobos and chimpanzees in captivity have shown surprising differences in their personalities. When placed in a zoo, bonobos are generally calm and relaxed. They seem to enjoy their surroundings and are playful and cooperative with researchers. However, chimpanzees act much more aggressively than bonobos when placed in similar situations. They are unwilling to work with scientists and easily become angry. Chimpanzees have even been known to break out of their cages and destroy expensive scientific equipment. These findings strongly suggest that bonobos are much less aggressive than chimpanzees.

Another way in which the animals differ is in how they interact with one another. Bonobos generally live in harmony with the other members of their group. This is illustrated by the fact that larger bonobos almost never attack smaller ones. Even when they have intense conflicts, bonobos rarely become aggressive with one another. On the other hand, chimpanzees frequently resort to physical violence to resolve arguments, and larger male chimpanzees often attack smaller males to maintain control of their group. In short, chimpanzees rely on aggressive behavior much more than nonviolent bonobos.

## | Paraphrasing | The following sentences come from the reading passage. Complete each paraphrase with appropriate words or phrases.

1   Observations of bonobos and chimpanzees in captivity have shown surprising differences in their personalities.

→ *Scientists have found that bonobos and chimpanzees* _____ *when they are*

_____ .

2   These findings strongly suggest that bonobos are much less aggressive than chimpanzees.

→ *Unlike chimpanzees, which are* _____ *, bonobos are*

_____ .

3   Even when they have intense conflicts, bonobos rarely become aggressive with one another.

→ *Bonobos are not* _____ *even when they have arguments.*

4   Chimpanzees frequently resort to physical violence to resolve arguments.

→ *Chimpanzees rely on* _____ *in order to* _____ .


## | Summarizing | Complete the summary below by using the information from the reading passage. Be sure to paraphrase the information.

The reading passage mainly deals with the differences in behavior _____ . The passage gives two supporting ideas to support this claim. First, the passage explains that chimpanzees act _____ when they are being kept in zoos. The example given that illustrates this idea is the fact that bonobos _____ while chimpanzees do not. Second, the passage talks about how _____ animals than chimpanzees. The passage shows this by explaining that chimpanzees _____ whereas bonobos do not.

## 🔊 Vocabulary  Take a few moments to review the vocabulary items that will appear in this task.

**primate**  *n.* an animal such as a monkey, an ape, or a human being
Most **primates** have hair all over their bodies and walk on all fours.

**react**  *v.* to act in return to something; to respond
Do you know how to **react** when there is an emergency?

**conclude**  *v.* to reach a decision about; to decide
After talking with my friends, I **concluded** that I would stay home instead of going on vacation.

**invalid**  *adj.* not based on the truth; worthless
Your opinions are **invalid**.

**zoologist**  *n.* a scientist who studies animals and animal life
My sister loves animals, so she is studying to become a **zoologist**.

**creature**  *n.* a living being, especially an animal
The **creatures** on the Earth today are very different from the ones that lived here five million years ago.

**shocking**  *adj.* very surprising; outrageous
Her rude comments were very **shocking** to me.

**tranquil**  *adj.* calm; peaceful
I love visiting the forest because it is so clean and **tranquil**.

## Listening

Now listen to part of a lecture on the topic you just read about.

02-01

**| Paraphrasing |** The following sentences come from the lecture. Complete each paraphrase with appropriate words or phrases.

1   Studies of bonobos have shown them to be less aggressive than chimps but only when they are both in captivity.

→ *Research done on bonobos in captivity has shown them to be* _____ *than chimpanzees.*

2   In other words, these experiments are invalid because they don't compare how bonobos and chimps act in the wild.

→ *Because they do not compare the way bonobos and chimpanzees act* _____ , *these studies are not valid.*

3   For a long time, zoologists thought that bonobos lived in peace and avoided direct conflict.

→ *Zoologists long believed that bonobos were* _____ *that did not* _____ .

4   The reason that researchers had not discovered this sooner is that the smaller bonobos only attack when there are no other creatures around.

→ *Scientists only recently learned about this because* _____ *only attack when they are alone* _____ .


**| Summarizing |** Complete the summary below by using the information from the lecture. Be sure to paraphrase the information.

The professor's lecture explains that bonobos may not be as peaceful as _____ .
She gives two supporting ideas to support her thesis. First, she mentions that _____
according to _____ . She explains that because studies of bonobos and chimpanzees
have only observed _____ , they are not valid. Second, she talks about how bonobos
interact with one another by saying that _____ previously thought. To explain this idea,
the professor talks about new research which has found that smaller bonobos _____
when they are _____ .

## Tandem Note-Taking

Refer to the paraphrasing and summarizing exercises to complete the side-by-side notes below. Include only the two points from the reading and the listening that clearly contract each other.

### READING

**Main Idea**

*Bonobos are usually*

*but chimpanzees are*

**First Supporting Argument**

*When they are in captivity, bonobos are*

*but chimpanzees act much more*

Supporting Detail

**Second Supporting Argument**

*Bonobos live*

*while chimpanzees*

Supporting Detail

### LISTENING

**Main Idea**

*There might be other explanations for*

**First Supporting Argument**

*Animals behave differently depending on*

Supporting Detail

**Second Supporting Argument**

*Bonobos may not*

Supporting Detail

Use this page to write your response. You have 20 minutes to complete your essay.

| Writing Guide | Summarize the points made in the lecture, being sure to explain how they cast doubt on specific points made in the reading passage. |
|---|---|
| **First Paragraph** ○<br><br>State and discuss thesis | |
| **Second Paragraph** ○<br><br>First main idea from lecture<br><br>Supporting detail<br><br>Contradiction from reading | |
| **Third Paragraph** ○<br><br>Second main idea from lecture<br><br>Supporting detail<br><br>Contradiction from reading | |
| **Fourth Paragraph** ○<br><br>Conclusion (optional) | |

🔊 **Scaffolding**   Here are some useful phrases to help you when you write.

> The reading passage and the lecture compare…

> Her arguments cast doubt on the claims made in…

> The instructor begins her lecture by explaining…

> This challenges the reading's assertion that…

> Next, the professor states that…

> She illustrates this by mentioning…

> This argument challenges the claim made in the reading passage that…

The reading passage and the lecture compare bonobos with chimpanzees. The reading passage suggests that bonobos are much more peaceful than chimpanzees, but the professor's lecture casts doubt on this claim.

The instructor begins her lecture by explaining that animals change the way they act to adapt to their situations. She talks about how this relates to studies of bonobos and chimpanzees. Because these studies only focused on animals in captivity, they are invalid since they do not explain how bonobos and chimpanzees act in the wild. The professor's argument calls into question the reading passage's assertion that bonobos are less aggressive than chimpanzees.

Next, the lecturer talks about how bonobos may not live in total harmony with one another. She says that zoologists had believed that bonobos were peaceful animals. However, they have recently discovered that smaller bonobos actually attack larger bonobos. Scientists did not learn about this sooner because the smaller bonobos only attack where there is no one around. This argument challenges the claim made in the reading passage that bonobos are peaceful animals that do not resort to violence.

| **Critical Analysis** |   Refer to the sample response to complete the tasks below.

**1**   Underline the topic sentence in each paragraph.

**2**   Double underline the sentences that refer to the listening.

**3**   Which word in the response means "**worthless**"? Write the word on the line below.

_____

**4**   What does "**live in harmony**" mean? Find the sentence that explains this and write it on the lines below.

_____

_____

**5**   List at least two of the transitions the writer uses on the lines below.

_____

_____

_____

The lecture after the passage. Gives some disagreement for the text. There was said bonobos are peaceful. But lecture says this might not be truth.

Firstly, the passage says bonobos have, much more clam then the chimpanzees. The bonobos are playful and cooperative. Unlike the chimpanzees. This shows the bonobos are harmony animals. However, the arguements is made differently in lecture. Professor says both animals captivity. So they are invalid.

Nextly, it is reading that the bonobos are much more peaceful. **1** This is truth because, the large bonobos don't not attack the small ones. **2** So this way animals are different. In lecture, it says otherwise. **3** She mentions that bonobos lives harmony lives. But the bonobos sometimes attack each other. So the discovery says that bonobos are not so tranquil.

| **Critical Analysis** |   Refer to the sample response to complete the tasks below.

**1**   In which of the following ways should the highlighted sentences be rewritten?

   Ⓐ  According to the reading passage, it is not true that bonobos are peaceful.

   Ⓑ  Although the reading passage states that bonobos are peaceful, the lecturer questions this argument.

   Ⓒ  According to the lecture, the peacefulness of bonobos might not be true, which is unlike the reading.

**2**   Where should the following sentence be added to improve the response?

**On the other hand, chimpanzees often attack one another.**

   Ⓐ  **1**

   Ⓑ  **2**

   Ⓒ  **3**

**3**   Find at least two grammatical mistakes in the response. Write the corrected sentences on the lines below.

_____

_____

_____

# Teachers Should Update Their Knowledge Regularly

 Do you agree or disagree with the following statement? Teachers should be required to update their knowledge every five years. Use specific reasons and examples to support your answer.

## Generating Ideas

The following questions will help you write your response. Answer each with one or two sentences. Plan an answer for both options. Some ideas have been provided to help you.

### Idea Box   Agree

**1 Q** How can the philosophy of teaching change over time?

**A** *New teaching methods are developed all the time. Teachers need to know about them.*

**2 Q** How do students and schools benefit from requiring teachers to update their knowledge?

**A** *Students benefit*

**3 Q** What are some other jobs that require workers to update their knowledge regularly?

**A** *Some other jobs include*

Reason 1:

Reason 2:

### Idea Box   Disagree

**1 Q** How do teachers improve their teaching skills on a daily basis?

**A** *Teachers learn something new and improve their teaching skills every time they teach.*

**2 Q** What certification is required to become a professional teacher?

**A** *Teachers need*

**3 Q** What are some drawbacks to requiring teachers to update their knowledge regularly?

**A** *The new methods teachers learn*

Reason 1:

Reason 2:

## Developing Ideas

Having examined the two options, which do you feel more comfortable developing into an essay? Explain why you feel this way.

Use the outline to plan your response to the following: Do you agree or disagree with the following statement? Teachers should update their knowledge every five years. Use specific reasons and examples to support your answer.

### Agree

**Thesis Statement**

*I believe that teachers should be required to*

*update their knowledge every five years.*

**First Supporting Idea**

Supporting Example

**Second Supporting Idea**

Supporting Example

**Conclusion**

### Disagree

**Thesis Statement**

*I believe that teachers are capable of*

*improving their abilities on their own.*

**First Supporting Idea**

Supporting Example

**Second Supporting Idea**

Supporting Example

**Conclusion**

Use this page to write your response. You have 30 minutes to complete your essay.

| Writing Guide | Do you agree or disagree with the following statement? Teachers should be required to update their knowledge every five years. Use specific reasons and examples to support your answer. |
|---|---|
| **First Paragraph** ▷<br><br>State and discuss thesis<br><br><br>**Second Paragraph** ▷<br><br>First main supporting idea<br><br>Supporting detail<br><br>Example<br><br><br><br><br>**Third Paragraph** ▷<br><br>Second main supporting idea<br><br>Supporting detail<br><br>Example<br><br><br><br>**Fourth Paragraph** ▷<br><br>Conclusion | |

**Scaffolding** Here are some useful phrases to help you when you write.

- ❯ I agree/disagree that teachers need to…
- ❯ First of all, teachers are already…
- ❯ In contrast, teachers who…
- ❯ This means that all school teachers have…

- ❯ As a result of… teachers should be required to…
- ❯ In addition, teachers…
- ❯ To give you an idea, here is an example from…
- ❯ For the reasons illustrated above, it is clear that…

I disagree that teachers need to update their knowledge every five years for two reasons. One, teachers are certified educational professionals who are capable of improving their abilities on their own. Two, their teaching is evaluated by students, parents, and other teachers every day.

First of all, teachers are already certified experts. Becoming a teacher requires an education degree and years of training. In university education programs, potential teachers are taught how to create lesson plans, how to motivate students, and how to teach effectively. Once they graduate, these students have to pass state certification tests in order to obtain their teaching licenses. Passing these exams requires students to have a deep understanding of the subject they want to teach as well as various teaching methods to use in the classroom. This means that all school teachers have the training and knowledge needed to be effective educators. Therefore, requiring teachers to update their knowledge every few years is unnecessary.

In addition, teachers receive feedback on a daily basis. They are constantly being evaluated by students, parents, and other faculty members. Instructors who do not teach effectively are told about their shortcomings and are given the opportunity to correct them. For instance, my older sister is a teacher. During her first year of teaching, many of her students were not doing well in her classes. My sister was not sure about what to do, so she got some advice from the older, more experienced teachers at her school. As a result, her students' performances increased dramatically. Today, she is one of her school's top teachers. For educators like my sister, such experiences are much more instructive than any required teaching courses could ever be.

Teachers are certified education experts who receive feedback about their work every day. It is clear that teachers should not be required to update their knowledge because they already do so by themselves.

| **Critical Analysis** |   Refer to the sample response to complete the tasks below.

1    Underline the topic sentence in each paragraph.

2    Double underline the sentences that include supporting details.

3    List at least two of the examples the writer uses on the lines below.

_____

_____

_____

Today, alot of people worried about the quality of teachers. They think that teachers are not as good as they should. For because of this reason, teachers should update themself every five year.

First, the way of teaching the teacher know become out of date. What I mean is, the teaching knowledge is not sufficient new. So they have to update the knowledge. For example, the teacher graduate college many times ago. So what they know is too old. This teacher should become more updated for the students knowledge. Like my teacher is school. Her teaching way was too boring. So I could not learn so much. Therefore, she must update her knowledge. This is also true for each teachers.

Second, teachers might be too lazy. They think all ready know about teaching, so why so she bother to up grade the knowledge? People have to be tell what to do. And so they have to be made to do it. Like with teaching. If for example the teacher still doesn't computer in the class, it has to be used by the teacher. What I mean is, teacher should know about new teaching technike. The only way this happen if the teacher be forced to update their knowledge every five years.

In conclusion, teaching is too important. So teachers must know how to teach better. For this reasons, teacher should update their knowledge every five years.

| **Critical Analysis** | Refer to the sample response to complete the tasks below.

1   Which of the following sentences could be added to strengthen the response?

   Ⓐ If teachers do not know something, then they are not able to explain it very well.

   Ⓑ Studies show that teachers do not benefit from forced teacher training.

   Ⓒ Requiring teachers to update their knowledge will help them become more effective instructors.

2   The topic sentence from the first body paragraph is not clear. Rewrite it to make it clearer.

3   Think of at least one supporting idea to add to the second body paragraph to make it more interesting.

4   Find at least two grammatical mistakes in the response. Write the corrected sentences on the lines below.

# Part **B**

# History: **The Collapse of Egypt's Old Kingdom**

## Vocabulary Take a few moments to review the vocabulary items that will appear in this task.

**suffer** *v.* to experience something painful

If one of you makes a mistake, you will all have to **suffer**.

**unquestioned** *adj.* accepted without question

Richard's leadership was **unquestioned**.

**greedy** *adj.* wanting or taking all that one can get with no thought of what others need

Stop being so **greedy**. You already have a full plate of food.

**ambitious** *adj.* having a strong desire to be successful

In order to become president, you must be **ambitious**.

**challenge** *v.* to question; to face up to

No one was brave enough to **challenge** the school bully.

**destabilize** *v.* to weaken the power of a government

Fighting throughout the nation has **destabilized** the national government.

**demise** *n.* the end of the existence of someone or something; death

Downloading music over the Internet has led to the **demise** of CDs and cassette tapes.

**drought** *n.* a long period of no rain

During the **drought**, everyone was required to reduce the amount of water they used.

**irrigate** *v.* to water crops

We **irrigate** our crops with water from the stream.

**revolt** *n.* an attempt to overthrow the authority of the state; a rebellion

After all their complaints were ignored, the citizens staged a **revolt** against the government.

## Reading

Read the passage carefully. Try to understand what the main argument of the passage is. You have 3 minutes to read.

The Old Kingdom in ancient Egypt was the first of the three kingdom periods. It was a time of great wealth and development, during which the Great Pyramids were constructed. However, after centuries of continuous growth, Egypt suffered a series of terrible events that eventually led to the collapse of the Old Kingdom.

One of the key events that brought down the Old Kingdom was the weakening of the central government. Throughout most of this period, the rule of the pharaohs and the royal families was unquestioned. Over time, however, many new laws were made that lessened their influence throughout the nation. This caused regional governors to become greedy and ambitious. They started to challenge the leadership of the pharaohs. Civil wars began to occur as these governors sought more power. The resulting conflicts further weakened and destabilized the national government.

Another contributing factor to the demise of the Old Kingdom was a major drought that lasted for several decades. According to a historical document, Egypt suffered a severe decrease in rainfall that lasted almost fifty years. This was especially troubling because Egyptian farmers relied on floodwater from the Nile River to irrigate their crops. Naturally, the lack of rainfall prevented this from occurring. The subsequent food shortages led to many deaths and peasant revolts throughout Egypt. Over time, the pharaohs became unable to control their people. It is this that ultimately led to the collapse of the Old Kingdom.

---

**| Paraphrasing |**  The following sentences come from the reading passage. Rewrite each sentence in the spaces provided below.

1   Throughout most of this period, the rule of the pharaohs and the royal families was unquestioned.

→ *The power of the pharaohs and royal families was* _____ *of the Old*
*Kingdom.*

2   They started to challenge the leadership of the pharaohs.

→ *Local governors* _____ *the power of the central government.*

3   According to a historical document, Egypt suffered a severe decrease in rainfall that lasted almost fifty years.

→ *Evidence shows that a drought* _____ *occurred in Egypt at this time.*

4   The subsequent food shortages led to many deaths and peasant revolts throughout Egypt.

→ *A lack of food resulted in* _____ *by citizens around the nation.*

**| Summarizing |**  Complete the summary below by using the information from the reading passage. Be sure to paraphrase the information.

The reading passage focuses on the events that caused _____ of Egypt's Old

Kingdom. The passage includes two supporting arguments to explain this. First, the passage states that

the central government's _____ contributed to the collapse. This is supported by

the example of the regional governors who _____ of the pharaoh. Second, the

passage explains that _____ also brought down _____ . This is

illustrated by the fact that many peasant revolts occurred as a result of _____ caused

by _____ .

## Vocabulary
Take a few moments to review the vocabulary items that will appear in this task.

**widespread** *adj.* spread out over a large area; pervasive

The damage caused by the flooding has been **widespread**.

**influence** *n.* the power to act on or to affect people or things

Parents and friends have a great **influence** on the lives of children.

**loyal** *adj.* faithful to one's family, duty, country, or beliefs

Dogs are popular pets because they are **loyal** to their owners.

**command** *v.* to give orders to; to control

An army general **commands** thousands of troops.

**uprising** *n.* a rebellion against a government; a revolt

The **uprising** against the president grew to include almost every citizen in the nation.

**famine** *n.* an extreme shortage of food

Although **famines** used to be somewhat common, today, they are very rare.

**tremendous** *adj.* extremely large in amount, extent, or degree; enormous

Our company has spent a **tremendous** amount of time designing this skyscraper.

**adjacent** *adj.* close to; next to

The bus stop is **adjacent** to the subway station.

## Listening

Now listen to part of a lecture on the topic you just read about.

02-02

**| Paraphrasing |** The following sentences come from the lecture. Rewrite each sentence in the spaces provided below.

1 The pharaohs recognized the importance of maintaining connections between regional leaders and the royal family.

→ *The pharaohs understood that it was important to maintain a relationship between*

........................................................ .

2 Thus, there were no advantages for governors to stage revolts against the pharaohs.

→ ........................................................ *, local leaders would not* ........................................................ *the central*

*government.*

3 And then there's the common belief that a famine occurred during the final years of the Old Kingdom.

→ *Many people also think that* ........................................................ *happened during*

........................................................ .

4 Although this region was adjacent to Egypt, the weather in the two places was completely different.

→ *The climate in this area was* ........................................................ *even though the two places were located*

........................................................ .

**| Summarizing |** Complete the summary below by using the information from the lecture. Be sure to paraphrase the information.

The lecturer calls into question the arguments ........................................................ . He offers two pieces

of evidence to support his viewpoint. First, he explains that regional governors had little reason to

........................................................ . He believes this because the pharaoh ........................................................ and was

in command of ........................................................ . Second, the instructor states that there may not have actually

been ........................................................ . He claims that the historical document describing the drought is from

another region, which means that it is impossible to conclude that ........................................................ .

## Tandem Note-Taking

Refer to the paraphrasing and summarizing exercises to complete the side-by-side notes below. Include only the two points from the reading and the listening that clearly contract each other.

### READING

**Main Idea**

*A series of terrible events led to*

**First Supporting Argument**

*The central government became*

Supporting Detail

**Second Supporting Argument**

*Egypt suffered*

Supporting Detail

### LISTENING

**Main Idea**

*The Old Kingdom may not*

**First Supporting Argument**

*The central government was*

Supporting Detail

**Second Supporting Argument**

*There may not have been*

Supporting Detail

Use this page to write your response. You have 20 minutes to complete your essay.

| Writing Guide | Summarize the points made in the lecture, being sure to explain how they challenge specific arguments made in the reading passage. |
|---|---|
| **First Paragraph** ○<br><br>State and discuss thesis | |
| **Second Paragraph** ○<br><br>First main idea from lecture<br><br>Contradiction from reading<br><br>Supporting detail | |
| **Third Paragraph** ○<br><br>Second main idea from lecture<br><br>Contradiction from reading<br><br>Supporting detail | |
| **Fourth Paragraph** ○<br><br>Conclusion (optional) | |

**Scaffolding**    Here are some useful phrases to help you when you write.

> The reading passage and the lecture deal with the topic of…

> The professor calls into question the arguments…

> The first reason the reading passage gives…

> The lecturer concludes that…

> His arguments rebut the claim made in the reading passage that…

> Meanwhile, the professor explains that…

> What this means is that there is no evidence to support the claim that…

The reading passage's author is convinced that a series of terrible events resulted in the collapse of Egypt's Old Kingdom, yet the lecturer disagrees that this was the main reason for its downfall.

The first reason that the reading passage gives for the downfall of the Old Kingdom is the weakening of Egypt's central government. The reading mentions that the pharaohs lost power over time and that local governors started civil wars as a result. Meanwhile, the professor explains that the pharaohs were still influential even though they had lost some of their power. He concludes that these leaders would not have gained anything by challenging the rule of the pharaohs.

The reading passage's author also believes that a severe drought contributed to the fall of the Old Kingdom. The reason is that the lack of rainfall led to widespread food shortages and peasant revolts. However, the lecturer explains that the historical document about the drought was not written in Egypt. Instead, it was from a region east of Egypt that had completely different weather. This means that there is no evidence to support the claim that the Old Kingdom collapsed because of a severe drought.

| **Critical Analysis** |   Refer to the sample response to complete the tasks below.

**1**   Underline the topic sentence in each paragraph.

**2**   Double underline the sentences that refer to the listening.

**3**   Which word in the response means "**questioning**"? Write the word on the line below.

_____

**4**   What does "**drought**" mean? Find the sentence that explains this and write it on the lines below.

_____

_____

**5**   List at least two of the transitions the writer uses on the lines below.

_____

_____

_____

the paragraph talk about old kingdom Egypt. it say old kingdom was finish, because of a series of terrible events. the lecture does not agree this.

in the beggining the reading was weak government. it say the pharaoh was unquestioned. so his power was stay the same. but the royal governers were so greedy. so they became power. but this is not true. in the listening. there say the pharaoh was an army. therefore no reason to worry.

also, it was talked about a severe decrise in rain fall. the Nile it was flood. but this time it was not. So it lead too many deaths throughout Egypt. **1** he say the documant was may be not true about Egypt. **2** there is say the document explained Egypt. **3**

the paragraph and listening talked about old kingdom. but they said very different things to disagremant.

| **Critical Analysis** |    Refer to the sample response to complete the tasks below.

1    In which of the following ways should the highlighted sentence be rewritten?

    Ⓐ  In the first part of the Old Kingdom, the government was weaker in the reading.

    Ⓑ  The reading first explains that Egypt's government became weaker over time.

    Ⓒ  The weakness of the government was not a problem according to the passage.

2    Where should the following sentence be added to improve the response?

**Again, the lecturer disagrees with the author of the reading passage.**

    Ⓐ  **1**

    Ⓑ  **2**

    Ⓒ  **3**

3    Find at least two grammatical mistakes in the response. Write the corrected sentences on the lines below.

_____

_____

_____

# Sometimes It Is Better Not to Say Anything

Do you agree or disagree with the following statement? If you cannot say anything nice, it is better not to say anything at all. Use specific reasons and examples to support your answer.

## Generating Ideas

The following questions will help you write your response. Answer each with one or two sentences. Plan an answer for both options. Some ideas have been provided to help you.

---

**Idea Box    Agree**

**1 Q** How can saying things that are not nice affect other people's feelings?

**A** *Saying things that are not nice usually makes people angry and upset.*

**2 Q** How can it be good for people to think they are fine when they really are not?

**A** *When people do not know about their problems, they are*

**3 Q** What are some instances when it is not okay to say something critical?

**A** *You should never say something critical when*

---

Reason 1:

Reason 2:

---

**Idea Box    Disagree**

**1 Q** How can saying things that are not nice help other people improve themselves?

**A** *Saying things that are not nice can make people understand and fix their problems.*

**2 Q** How can it be bad for people to think they are fine when they really are not?

**A** *If people do not know about their problems, then*

**3 Q** What are some instances when it is okay to say something critical?

**A** *You should say something critical when*

---

Reason 1:

Reason 2:

---

## Developing Ideas

Having examined the two options, which do you feel more comfortable developing into an essay? Explain why you feel this way.

Use the outline to plan your response to the following: Do you agree or disagree with the following statement? If you cannot say anything nice, it is better not to say anything at all. Use specific reasons and examples to support your answer.

| Agree | Disagree |
|---|---|
| **Thesis Statement** | **Thesis Statement** |
| *I feel that if you cannot say anything nice, then it is better not to say anything at all.* | *I believe that saying something that is a bit mean or critical is sometimes beneficial.* |
| **First Supporting Idea** | **First Supporting Idea** |
| | |
| Supporting Example | Supporting Example |
| | |
| **Second Supporting Idea** | **Second Supporting Idea** |
| | |
| Supporting Example | Supporting Example |
| | |
| **Conclusion** | **Conclusion** |
| | |

Use this page to write your response. You have 30 minutes to complete your essay.

| Writing Guide | Do you agree or disagree with the following statement? If you cannot say anything nice, it is better not to say anything at all. Use specific reasons and examples to support your answer. |
| --- | --- |
| **First Paragraph** ○<br><br>State and discuss thesis | |
| **Second Paragraph** ○<br><br>First main supporting idea<br><br>Supporting detail<br><br>Example | |
| **Third Paragraph** ○<br><br>Second main supporting idea<br><br>Supporting detail<br><br>Example | |
| **Fourth Paragraph** ○<br><br>Conclusion | |

**Scaffolding**   Here are some useful phrases to help you when you write.

> Many people today worry about…

> As for me, I still believe that it is better to…

> To begin with, people often…

> To illustrate, I will give a personal…

> There are also times when saying something…

> For instance, I once told a friend that…

> After I said that, my friend…

> I believe that it is generally better to… than…

These days, people are quick to express their opinions no matter what they think. They say whatever comes to mind without considering the impact their words will have on others. As for me, I still believe that if you can't say anything nice, it is better not to say anything at all.

To begin with, people often say mean things that are not constructive and only hurt the feelings of others. By saying these things, they only cause problems. To illustrate, I will give a personal example. When I was in high school, I had a friend who was severely overweight. Although her weight problem was obvious, my friend was in denial about it. One day, she asked me if I thought she was getting too heavy. I told her that she was too fat and that she should lose about twenty kilograms. She immediately began crying and ran away from me. After that, she never spoke to me again. In this situation, saying something nice, even if it had been a lie, would have been a much better idea.

There are also times when saying something critical can worsen a situation for everyone involved. Some people, particularly those who are in power, do not want to hear bad news and would rather hear lies. This was the case at one of my part-time summer jobs. The manager at my store had a serious case of bad breath, but nobody was brave enough to tell him. Eventually, one of my co-workers told the manager about his problem. Even though my co-worker was trying to be helpful, the manager became furious. He made everybody do extra work for the rest of the month and was very mean to all of us. If none of us had said anything, this situation would not have happened.

In conclusion, I contend that there are certain situations when it is better to not tell the truth. Saying things that are mean or critical can make people upset with you, and being honest can cause a situation to become worse.

---

**| Critical Analysis |**   Refer to the sample response to complete the tasks below.

**1**   Underline the topic sentence in each paragraph.

**2**   Double underline the sentences that include supporting details.

**3**   List at least two of the examples the writer uses on the lines below.

_____

_____

_____

These days, some people are worrying about saying too mean things. They worry about making other's too angry. This is also when they talk to other people. I however, believe that saying something mean is sometimes nessesseary.

The first reason I believe this way is because say something not nice can make others get better. Like for instance, if your friend has a food in their teeth, it should be said about. If you don't saying anything, then that people will not know about the food in the teeth. So they go about with food in their mouths and its too ugly. So other people say about the food in the mouth. Then they say mean things but in sectretly. So really you should only tell your friend about the food in their mouth. Its not too nice to say maybe; but it helps them become more better quickly.

The second reading I believe this way is makeing the situations get better. If you don't saying any thing, then no one will be chaning it, too. In this way, it is better to become criticize. Such as if you are working and you see a problem. No one elese is seeing it but only you. So you need to speak up, if you do, then the problem gets solution. However, when you are sillent nothing getting improvement. So in this way, you should speak up.

When there are sensitivy situion, you need to say something nice. Other times is better to say something mean. Therfore I disagree with the question given aboue.

---

| **Critical Analysis** | Refer to the sample response to complete the tasks below.

1   Where could the following sentence be added to strengthen the response?

**By telling my friend about her rude manners, she was able to become a more polite person.**

   (A) Body paragraph 1

   (B) Body paragraph 2

   (C) Final paragraph

2   The topic sentence from the second body paragraph is not clear. Rewrite it to make it clearer.

3   Think of at least one supporting idea to add to the second body paragraph to make it more interesting.

4   Find at least two grammatical mistakes in the response. Write the corrected sentences on the lines below.

# Part **B**

# Biology: **Yawning Lowers Blood Temperature**

## 🔊 **Vocabulary**   Take a few moments to review the vocabulary items that will appear in this task.

**theory**  *n.* a set of ideas created to explain why something happens

I am not sure who stole my candy, but I have a **theory**.

**propose**  *v.* to make a suggestion

Lawmakers **proposed** lowering the drinking age from twenty-one to eighteen.

**proven**  *adj.* known to be true

When a theory is finally **proven**, it is considered to be a fact.

**inactivity**  *n.* the state of being idle; not doing an activity

Avoid **inactivity** by keeping busy at all times.

**dramatically**  *adv.* to a great degree or large amount

It was cold in December, but it got **dramatically** colder in January.

**focused**  *adj.* concentrating on something

To do well on the exam, you have to remain **focused**.

**draw in**  *phr v.* to breathe in deeply; to take in

When we got to the top of the mountain, we **drew in** as much of the clean air as we could.

**regulate**  *v.* to control an activity, usually with a set of rules

Only the government can **regulate** the nation's road systems.

**generate**  *v.* to produce; to make

One purpose of river dams is to **generate** electricity.

**efficiently**  *adv.* proficiently; effectively

In order to finish the project by five o'clock, we need to work **efficiently**.

## Reading

Read the passage carefully. Try to understand what the main argument of the passage is. You have 3 minutes to read.

Throughout the centuries, several theories about the causes of yawning have been proposed, but none of them has ever been proved. This is no longer the case. Thanks to recent discoveries, scientists are starting to understand the reasons why a person yawns.

One reason that a person yawns has to do with oxygen levels in the brain. During periods of inactivity, the amount of oxygen in the brain can drop dramatically. This makes it difficult to concentrate. To remain focused, a person will yawn to draw in oxygen to remove carbon dioxide from the brain. This was proved in one recent study during which scientists compared the test scores of students who yawn before taking tests to those of students who do not. The researchers found that the yawning students had test scores that averaged five percent higher than the non-yawning students. These results suggest that yawning is an important aid for concentration.

Another purpose of yawning is that it helps to regulate the brain's blood temperature. In many ways, a person's brain is much like a personal computer. They both generate a great amount of heat, and they both function more efficiently when they are cooler. This is why a person yawns when concentrating on something. Yawning brings cooler blood into the brain from other parts of the body. This lowers the temperature of the brain. As a result, an individual is able to concentrate more effectively. Therefore, a person must yawn in order to make the brain function properly.

| Paraphrasing | The following sentences come from the reading passage. Complete each paraphrase with appropriate words or phrases.

1   During periods of inactivity, the amount of oxygen in the brain can drop dramatically.

→ *The brain's oxygen levels* _____ *when we* _____ .

2   To remain focused, a person will yawn to draw in oxygen to remove carbon dioxide from the brain.

→ *By yawning, people are* _____ *by bringing in*

_____ *and getting rid of* _____ *in the brain.*

3   The researchers found that the yawning students had test scores that averaged five percent higher than the non-yawning students.

→ *According to the study, test scores of* _____ *were*

_____ *than those who did not yawn.*

4   Yawning brings cooler blood into the brain from other parts of the body.

→ *When people yawn, they move* _____ *from other parts of their bodies to*

_____ .

| Summarizing | Complete the summary below by using the information from the reading passage. Be sure to paraphrase the information.

The main topic of the reading passage is _____ . The author presents two supporting

theories. The first is that yawning helps _____ . According to the example, yawning

helps students perform better on tests. The next argument is that yawning _____ .

The passage states that people bring _____ when they yawn. In turn, this helps them

concentrate more easily.

## 🔊 Vocabulary
Take a few moments to review the vocabulary items that will appear in this task.

**mystery** *n.* something that is not known or explained or that is kept secret

Even many years after the murder happened, the identity of the killer remained a **mystery**.

**convincing** *adj.* causing one to believe that something is true; persuasive

I will not believe your story unless you give me some **convincing** facts to support it.

**determine** *v.* to decide something

Doctors were unable to **determine** what had caused his illness.

**conduct** *v.* to organize and do a task

The police **conducted** a search for the missing children.

**increase** *v.* to become larger in size, number, or amount

The number of people living in the world **increases** each year.

**decrease** *v.* to become smaller in size, number, or amount

In order to lose weight, you must **decrease** the amount of food you eat.

**frequency** *n.* the number of times something happens in a specific amount of time

Car accidents increase in **frequency** during the winter.

**result** *n.* something that comes about as an effect or end

How you conduct an experiment is important, but it is the **results** that matter the most.

## Listening

Now listen to part of a lecture on the topic you just read about.

02-03

**| Paraphrasing |** The following sentences come from the lecture. Complete each paraphrase with appropriate words or phrases.

1   Scientists have conducted experiments to determine whether changes in oxygen levels cause people to yawn.

→ *Researchers have performed studies* _____ *is caused by differences in*

_____ .

2   What they found was that the frequency of yawning by the participants did not change at all.

→ *They discovered that* _____ *participants yawned*

_____ .

3   They first determined the number of times most people yawn on average.

→ *The scientists began by calculating* _____ *yawn.*

4   From these results, we can conclude that yawning does little to regulate the brain's temperature.

→ *Based on these findings, it is safe to say that* _____ *is not affected by*

*yawning.*

**| Summarizing |** Complete the summary below by using the information from the lecture. Be sure to paraphrase the information.

In the lecture, the professor argues that the _____ is still not understood. To

explain this, she gives two reasons. The instructor mentions that yawning does not seem to affect

_____ . Scientists found that _____ levels did not cause people

to yawn more or less often. The lecturer moves on to discuss how yawning can _____ .

According to a study, people do not _____ on hot days. This suggests that the brain's

temperature is not affected by yawning.

Refer to the paraphrasing and summarizing exercises to complete the side-by-side notes below. Include only the two points from the reading and the listening that clearly contract each other.

**Main Idea**

*Thanks to recent discoveries, scientists*

**First Supporting Argument**

*One cause for a person to yawn deals with*

Supporting Detail

**Second Supporting Argument**

*Another purpose of yawning is that it helps*

Supporting Detail

**Main Idea**

*None of the claims about the causes of*

*yawning*

**First Supporting Argument**

*According to recent studies, oxygen levels*

Supporting Detail

**Second Supporting Argument**

*Furthermore, yawning may not*

Supporting Detail

Use this page to write your response. You have 20 minutes to complete your essay.

| Writing Guide | Summarize the points made in the lecture, being sure to explain how they challenge specific claims made in the reading passage. |
|---|---|
| **First Paragraph** ○<br><br>State and discuss thesis<br><br>**Second Paragraph** ○<br><br>First main idea from lecture<br><br>Supporting detail<br><br>Contradiction from reading<br><br>**Third Paragraph** ○<br><br>Second main idea from lecture<br><br>Supporting detail<br><br>Contradiction from reading<br><br>**Fourth Paragraph** ○<br><br>Conclusion (optional) | |

**🔧 Scaffolding**  Here are some useful phrases to help you when you write.

> The topic of the reading passage and the lecture is…

> The reading passage argues that… but the arguments presented by the lecturer…

> First, the professor states that…

> She mentions an experiment where…

> These findings go against the argument made in the reading passage that…

> The instructor then goes on to argue that…

> This contradicts the idea that… which was the argument made in the reading passage.

The topic of the reading passage and the lecture is yawning. The reading passage argues that yawning controls brain activity, but the arguments presented by the lecturer call these findings into question.

First, the professor states that yawning does not affect the brain's oxygen levels. She mentions an experiment during which scientists placed subjects in a room and changed the levels of oxygen and carbon dioxide. The researchers discovered that the number of times the subjects yawned did not change. This implied that low oxygen levels do not cause yawning. These findings go against the argument made in the reading passage that people yawn in order to increase oxygen levels in their brains.

The instructor then goes on to argue that yawning does not affect the brain's temperature. She talks about an experiment that measured the number of times people yawn on normal days and on hot days. The scientists found that people do not yawn more often when the weather is warmer. This suggests that temperature changes do not cause people to yawn. This contradicts the idea that yawning helps cool the brain, which is the argument presented in the reading passage.

| Critical Analysis |   Refer to the sample response to complete the tasks below.

**1**   Underline the topic sentence in each paragraph.

**2**   Double underline the sentences that refer to the listening.

**3**   Which word in the response means "**go up in number**"? Write the word on the line below.

_____

**4**   What does "**contradict**" mean? Find the sentence that explains this and write it on the lines below.

_____

_____

**5**   List at least two of the transitions the writer uses on the lines below.

_____

_____

_____

In reading passage it was said about the yawning. There it was said the yawning has theory. It the lecture it was said untrue.

Once it was said the yawning make oxygen levels the brain. This because the yawning draw oxygen and remove carbon dioxide. So we think clearer. In fact, yawning helps the students taking the test. But otherwise the yawning does not do this. Maybe the yawning does not helping the test.

Nextly, the yawning is the brain's blood temperature, because our brain is a personal computer. We need it to concentrate. So we yawn when its too warm. **1** But we do not have to yawning more frequently. **2** The professor say this is so. **3** So maybe it cannot be trust.

In conclusion, yawn might be good for body it might not be good. It depends.

---

| **Critical Analysis** |   Refer to the sample response to complete the tasks below.

1   In which of the following ways should the highlighted sentences be combined?

    Ⓐ   When we yawn, it gets rid of the oxygen and the carbon dioxide in the brain, so we are less able to concentrate.

    Ⓑ   Because our brains lack oxygen and have too much carbon dioxide, we have to think more clearly when we yawn.

    Ⓒ   Yawning draws in oxygen and removes carbon dioxide from the brain, and this allows us to think more clearly.

2   Where should the following sentence be added to improve the response?

**However, if this were true, people would have to yawn more frequently on hot days.**

    Ⓐ   **1**

    Ⓑ   **2**

    Ⓒ   **3**

3   Find at least two grammatical mistakes in the response. Write the corrected sentences on the lines below.

_____

_____

_____

# Looks Are More Important than Ideas

Do you agree or disagree with the following statement? How people look or dress is more important for success than having good ideas. Use specific reasons and examples to support your answer.

## Generating Ideas

The following questions will help you write your response. Answer each with one or two sentences. Plan an answer for both options. Some ideas have been provided to help you.

### Idea Box  Agree

**1 Q** What judgments do people make about other people based on their appearance?

**A** *People may think an attractive person is smarter than a person who is less attractive.*

**2 Q** Do you think people who are more attractive get treated differently? Explain.

**A** *Those who are more attractive are*

**3 Q** What are some jobs in which looking good is important?

**A** *Some of those jobs include*

Reason 1:

Reason 2:

### Idea Box  Disagree

**1 Q** If somebody is too attractive, how might other people feel?

**A** *When somebody is too attractive, other people may feel jealous and angry.*

**2 Q** What are some jobs in which good ideas are more important than good looks?

**A** *Jobs where good ideas are more important are*

**3 Q** Who are some of the most successful people in the world? How do these people look?

**A** *Some very successful include*

Reason 1:

Reason 2:

## Developing Ideas

Having examined the two options, which do you feel more comfortable developing into an essay? Explain why you feel this way.

Use the outline to plan your response to the following: Do you agree or disagree with the following statement? How people look or dress is more important for success than having good ideas. Use specific reasons and examples to support your answer.

| Agree | Disagree |
|---|---|
| **Thesis Statement** | **Thesis Statement** |
| *I agree that good looks are more important than good ideas.* | *Although looking good is important, I feel that having good ideas is more important.* |
| **First Supporting Idea** | **First Supporting Idea** |
| Supporting Example | Supporting Example |
| **Second Supporting Idea** | **Second Supporting Idea** |
| Supporting Example | Supporting Example |
| **Conclusion** | **Conclusion** |

Use this page to write your response. You have 30 minutes to complete your essay.

| Writing Guide | Do you agree or disagree with the following statement? How people look or dress is more important for success than having good ideas. Use specific reasons and examples to support your answer. |
|---|---|
| **First Paragraph** ○<br><br>State and discuss thesis<br><br>**Second Paragraph** ○<br><br>First main supporting idea<br><br>Supporting detail<br><br>Example<br><br>**Third Paragraph** ○<br><br>Second main supporting idea<br><br>Supporting detail<br><br>Example<br><br>**Fourth Paragraph** ○<br><br>Conclusion | |

**Scaffolding**   Here are some useful phrases to help you when you write.

- It is said that first impressions are…
- Taking this into consideration, it becomes evident that…
- One reason that looking good is important is…
- According to research, people…

- In order to be successful in the business world…
- On top of this, good looks…
- Consider the case of…
- Conversely, people who do not look good…
- For this reason, it is clear that…

It is said that first impressions are the most important. Whenever we first meet people, we make many assumptions about them based on their appearance. Oftentimes, these assumptions stay with us long afterward even if they are not true. Taking this into consideration, it becomes evident that looking good is more important for success than having good ideas.

One reason that looking good is so critical for success is that our society values attractiveness so much. In magazines and on television, you see only the most attractive people and the good things they do. At the same time, you see advertisements for fashion, weight-loss programs, and plastic surgery. These services exist because people want to look their best. They feel this way for good reason. According to research, people formulate opinions of others based solely on their looks. We make inferences about people's intelligence, educational attainment, and personality based on their appearance. In order to be taken seriously in the business world, looking good is essential.

Even after we have made our first impression, being attractive remains important. The reason is that people are more willing to listen to and help people who are more attractive. This is also why the most successful people are often attractive. To give an example, recent surveys have found that people who are tall, thin, and attractive earn nearly ten percent more than those who are average looking. In fields where looks are important, the income gap is even greater. On top of this, the study also found that people who look below average earn fifteen percent less money than people of average attractiveness. Considering this, it becomes evident that people who are more attractive are more successful.

In summary, it is clear that being successful requires good looks. People who are more attractive are more respected and earn more money. For this reason, one cannot be successful without putting some emphasis on appearance.

**| Critical Analysis |** Refer to the sample response to complete the tasks below.

**1** Underline the topic sentence in each paragraph.

**2** Double underline the sentences that include supporting details.

**3** List at least two of the examples the writer uses on the lines below.

_____

_____

_____

The question above says that how people look or dress is more important for success than having good ideas. Although some people may agree with this. I don't agree that looks are more important, than good ideas.

One reason I feel this way, is many jobs require good ideas. Think about inventer, doctor, scientist, etc. These jobs, don't need good looking employee. They just have to have good ideals. For instance, the scientist how dress nice, if he has no good idea, then his working becomes the problem. Some jobs, Its' just not a good idea.

Second reason I feel this way, become sometimes looking good makes people jealisly. They can't look as good, so they feel angry. Think about when you have a good looks co worker. You can't think about you as well, so you become jealisly. Sometimes, having the good looks co worker is not always good.

The final reason is that not handsome people have successful. Most of people who are rich are not looking well. They make fortune, from big ideas not form looks. Consider the Bill Gates, Werren Buffit, etc. Those guys have been success without being atracttive.

Sometimes, looking good is too important. Otherwise it does not mater. If you have the good ideas then the success come naturally.

| Critical Analysis | Refer to the sample response to complete the tasks below.

1   Which of the following sentences could be added to strengthen the response?
    Ⓐ Some jobs put greater importance on good ideas while others stress good looks.
    Ⓑ The people who dress the best are usually the most successful.
    Ⓒ The wealthiest people in the world became successful because of their ideas.

2   The topic sentence from the third body paragraph is not clear. Rewrite it to make it clearer.

3   Think of at least one supporting idea to add to the second body paragraph to make it more interesting.

4   Find at least two grammatical mistakes in the response. Write the corrected sentences on the lines below.

_____

_____

_____

# Part **B**

# Education: **Higher Education Should Be Free**

## 🔊 **Vocabulary** Take a few moments to review the vocabulary items that will appear in this task.

**skyrocket** *v.* suddenly to increase by a very large amount

Sales of those sneakers **skyrocketed** after LeBron James started wearing them.

**insist** *v.* to demand or say in a strong, firm manner

If you are going to stay in my house, I **insist** that you come home by midnight every night.

**tuition** *n.* money paid for education, especially at a college or university

The **tuition** at my university has nearly doubled over the past few years.

**follow suit** *phr v.* to do as someone else has done; to imitate

After our city made spitting illegal, other cities around the nation **followed suit**.

**developed nation** *n.* a nation with a high level of economic development

The United States, Canada, Japan, Korea, and most countries in Europe are **developed nations**.

**run into** *phr v.* to cost a lot of money

My mother's hospital bills **ran into** the tens of thousands of dollars following her accident.

**unattainable** *adj.* not able to be reached; not available

Your goals will remain **unattainable** if you do not work to reach them.

**deserve** *v.* to be worthy of; to earn

You **deserve** a vacation for all the hard work you have done for our company.

**indirect** *adj.* not straight; by a longer way

The government's new plan has both direct and **indirect** benefits.

**contribute** *v.* to work together with others to achieve a common goal

If our school needs money, then I will be glad to **contribute**.

## Reading

Read the passage carefully. Try to understand what the main argument of the passage is. You have 3 minutes to read.

With college tuition fees skyrocketing, students and parents across the nation are insisting that higher education become more affordable. Many nations throughout Europe offer free tuition at their universities. It is time for American schools to follow suit.

In today's competitive society, developed nations have a responsibility to educate their citizens. A nation's ability to compete depends largely on the number of college graduates it has. It is for this reason that several European nations provide all qualified students with a free university education. This is certainly not the case in the United States. In the U.S., tuition for just one semester can cost tens of thousands of dollars. This makes higher education unattainable for many qualified students. In order to make sure that all students get the education they deserve, universities must become tuition free.

Another advantage of no-cost higher education is the indirect benefits it brings. By making college education free, a greater number of people can become more educated. This, in turn, can benefit the overall community. Studies have shown that college graduates are more likely to contribute to their communities by donating money or by doing volunteer work. They are much more likely to participate in cultural events as well. Furthermore, cities with more college-educated people have lower crime rates. Thus, it is clear that in order to improve the quality of life for all citizens, higher education needs to be available at no cost.

---

**| Paraphrasing |** The following sentences come from the reading passage. Complete each paraphrase with appropriate words or phrases.

**1** In today's competitive society, developed nations have a responsibility to educate their citizens.

→ _____ *today must provide their people* _____ .

**2** This makes higher education unattainable for many qualified students.

→ *As result, a lot of* _____ *cannot afford* _____ .

**3** Studies have shown that college graduates are more likely to contribute to their communities by donating money or by doing volunteer work.

→ *Research shows that educated people more often donate* _____ *to their communities.*

**4** Thus, it is clear that in order to improve the quality of life for all citizens, higher education needs to be available at no cost.

→ *Higher education must be* _____ *in order to* _____ *for everybody.*

**| Summarizing |** Complete the summary below by using the information from the reading passage. Be sure to paraphrase the information.

The topic of the reading passage is _____ . The first reason the author gives is that wealthy nations must educate their citizens _____ . This is illustrated by the fact that most European nations already offer _____ to their citizens. Next, the reading passage states that providing free higher education brings _____ . These include greater participation in volunteer events and lower crime rates.

## 🔊 Vocabulary  Take a few moments to review the vocabulary items that will appear in this task.

**unintended**  *adj.* not meant to be done; unplanned

The building fire caused by the fireworks display was completely **unintended**.

**consequence**  *n.* something that happens as a result of an event

Every action has some sort of **consequence**.

**funding**  *n.* money given to pay for something specific

Since the state has reduced our **funding**, we are going to have to raise tuition.

**estimate**  *v.* to make a general but careful guess about the size, value, or cost of something

I do not know for sure how tall he is, but I **estimate** that he is about 190 centimeters tall.

**topnotch**  *adj.* of the highest quality; excellent

You can be sure that when you buy from us, you are getting only **topnotch** products.

**suitably**  *adv.* appropriately; correctly

The car was **suitably** luxurious as it cost several hundred thousand dollars.

**elsewhere**  *adv.* in other places; in another place

The servers at the restaurant were so rude. I think we should just start eating **elsewhere**.

---

## Listening

Now listen to part of a lecture on the topic you just read about.

02-04

**| Paraphrasing |** The following sentences come from the lecture. Complete each paraphrase with appropriate words or phrases.

**1** In fact, one recent study estimated that in order to provide all students with free higher education, the government would have to raise taxes by more than fifteen percent.

→ *Research shows that taxes would need to be increased by* _____ *to pay for free higher education.*

**2** Because of this, we can safely say that the public will not be willing to provide others with a free college education.

→ *Therefore, we can conclude that people will not pay for* _____ .

**3** Another less obvious consequence of providing free college educations would be a decrease in the quality of the instruction.

→ *A second drawback to* _____ *would be a reduction* _____ .

**4** If education were made free, then schools could no longer pay these talented instructors enough money.

→ *By making higher education no cost, universities could not afford to pay* _____ *high enough salaries.*

**| Summarizing |** Complete the summary below by using the information from the lecture. Be sure to paraphrase the information.

In the lecture, the professor talks about _____ of free higher education. One of these drawbacks is _____ . He explains that taxes would have to be raised by more than fifteen percent. The instructor also says that most Americans would not be willing to pay for something that does not _____ . Another drawback the lecturer talks about is the _____ of education. He explains that schools would not be able to _____ of their best instructors without charging tuition.

# Tandem Note-Taking

Refer to the paraphrasing and summarizing exercises to complete the side-by-side notes below. Include only the two points from the reading and the listening that clearly contract each other.

## READING

**Main Idea**

*To provide all qualified students with a higher education, American schools*

**First Supporting Argument**

*Developed nations have a responsibility to*

Supporting Detail

**Second Supporting Argument**

*Offering no-cost higher education also*

Supporting Detail

## LISTENING

**Main Idea**

*Although free higher education sounds like a great idea, it has*

**First Supporting Argument**

*Funding for tuition-free higher education must come from*

Supporting Detail

**Second Supporting Argument**

*Free higher education would decrease*

Supporting Detail

Use this page to write your response. You have 20 minutes to complete your essay.

| Writing Guide | Summarize the points made in the lecture, being sure to explain how they cast doubt on specific points made in the reading passage. |
|---|---|
| **First Paragraph** ▷<br><br>State and discuss thesis | |
| **Second Paragraph** ▷<br><br>First main idea from lecture<br><br>Contradiction from reading<br><br>Supporting detail | |
| **Third Paragraph** ▷<br><br>Second main idea from lecture<br><br>Contradiction from reading<br><br>Supporting detail | |
| **Fourth Paragraph** ▷<br><br>Conclusion (optional) | |

🌐 **Scaffolding**    Here are some useful phrases to help you when you write.

> The reading passage makes the argument that...

> To begin with, the reading passage states that...

> In this way, the instructor challenges the reading's argument that...

> However, the lecturer contends that...

> He illustrates this by mentioning...

> Next, to rebut the reading passage's claim that... the professor explains...

> His argument challenges the claim made in the reading passage that...

The reading passage makes the argument that American universities must provide free education to all students. The professor, however, believes that such a plan would have unintended consequences.

To begin with, the reading passage states that developed nations such as the United States have a responsibility to provide their citizens with a free university education. However, the lecturer contends that the government would have to raise taxes by more than fifteen percent to pay for free colleges. He then says that most American people do not want to cover the costs of a service they are not using themselves.

Next, to rebut the reading passage's argument that free higher education would provide benefits for everyone, the instructor explains how the quality of instruction would be affected. He says that good colleges charge high tuition in order to pay the salaries of professors. If universities cannot charge tuition, then they cannot pay their best professors enough money to stay. This would decrease the overall quality of a college education.

While the author of the reading passage wants higher education to become free, the professor argues against doing this.

---

| Critical Analysis | Refer to the sample response to complete the tasks below.

1   Underline the topic sentence in each paragraph.

2   Double underline the sentences that refer to the listening.

3   Which word in the response means "**unplanned**"? Write the word on the line below.

_____

4   What does "**cover the cost**" mean? Find the sentence that explains this and write it on the lines below.

_____

_____

5   List at least two of the transitions the writer uses on the lines below.

_____

_____

_____

The reading and the professor both talk about college. The reading argued that college should be free. The lecture argued that free college is not possibility.

**1** His first reason is that free college increses the taxes. **2** He says that pay for the college has to come from somewhere. **3** However, the Americans don't want to pay for something that they don't do, so it might not be able to do. The reading it was argued that free college has to be made, because other nations in Europe all ready have free college.

His next reason is that college should not be free because of the drop in education quality. The best colleges are the most expensive. They have to pay there professors a huge salaries. When college becomes free, they can't afford that. So the quality will become worse. This unlike the reading because there it said free colleges benefits the community. For example, free college makes the crime rates lower.

| **Critical Analysis** |   Refer to the sample response to complete the tasks below.

**1**   In which of the following ways should the highlighted sentences be rewritten?

   (A)   The author of the reading passage is in favor of free higher education while the lecturer is against it.

   (B)   The reading passage challenges the professor's argument that college should be made free.

   (C)   In the lecture, the professor presents reasons against those given in the reading passage.

**2**   Where should the following sentence be added to improve the response?

**He explains that taxes would have to be raised by more than fifteen percent to pay for free education.**

   (A)   **1**

   (B)   **2**

   (C)   **3**

**3**   Find at least two grammatical mistakes in the response. Write the corrected sentences on the lines below.

# Keeping Old Customs or Adopting New Ones

 When people move to another country, some of them decide to follow the customs of the new country. Others prefer to keep their own customs. Which one do you prefer and why? Use specific reasons and examples to support your choice.

## Generating Ideas

The following questions will help you write your response. Answer each with one or two sentences. Plan an answer for both options. Some ideas have been provided to help you.

### Idea Box   Follow New Customs

**1 Q** How can following the customs of the new country make it easier to integrate into society?

  **A** *It allows a person to understand the culture better, which makes it easier to make friends.*

**2 Q** How does following new customs make a person's life more comfortable?

  **A** *A person can*

**3 Q** What are some things a person can learn by adopting the customs of another country?

  **A** *Adopting new customs allows a person to*

Reason 1:

Reason 2:

### Idea Box   Keep Old Customs

**1 Q** How can keeping old customs make a person's life in a new country less stressful?

  **A** *By following the customs from home, a person can live life in the way that individual is used to.*

**2 Q** In what situations would a person not want to adopt the customs of a new country?

  **A** *A person may not adopt new customs when*

**3 Q** What are some factors that make it difficult for someone to adopt new customs quickly?

  **A** *Some of these include*

Reason 1:

Reason 2:

## Developing Ideas

Having examined the two options, which do you feel more comfortable developing into an essay? Explain why you feel this way.

Use the outline to plan your response to the following: When people move to another country, some of them decide to follow the customs of the new country. Others prefer to keep their own customs. Which one do you prefer and why? Use specific reasons and examples to support your choice.

| Follow New Customs | Keep Old Customs |
| --- | --- |
| **Thesis Statement** | **Thesis Statement** |
| *When you move to a new country, I feel it is better to adopt the customs of that nation.* | *I believe it is better for people to keep their own customs than to adopt those of another country.* |
| **First Supporting Idea** | **First Supporting Idea** |
| Supporting Example | Supporting Example |
| **Second Supporting Idea** | **Second Supporting Idea** |
| Supporting Example | Supporting Example |
| **Conclusion** | **Conclusion** |

Use this page to write your response. You have 30 minutes to complete your essay.

| Writing Guide | When people move to another country, some of them decide to follow the customs of the new country. Others prefer to keep their own customs. Which one do you prefer and why? Use specific reasons and examples to support your choice. |
|---|---|
| **First Paragraph** ○<br><br>State and discuss thesis | |
| **Second Paragraph** ○<br><br>First main supporting idea<br><br>Supporting detail<br><br>Example | |
| **Third Paragraph** ○<br><br>Second main supporting idea<br><br>Supporting detail<br><br>Example | |
| **Fourth Paragraph** ○<br><br>Conclusion | |

**Scaffolding**    Here are some useful phrases to help you when you write.

> Some people prefer to hold on to the customs of their…

> However, I feel their actions are…

> One reason to adopt the customs of a new country/keep old customs is…

> Let me give you a personal example to…

> Oftentimes, it is easier for people to…

> People who follow the local customs…

> For instance, when my family moved to…

> Although some people may prefer to cling to their old ways/adopt new customs, I think it is much better to…

Some people who move to another country prefer to hold on to the customs of their native lands. However, I feel that their actions are improper. When living in a new country, I believe it is essential to adopt the customs of the new country.

One reason to adopt the customs of a new country is that they allow you to live your life differently. For me, learning about and embracing different ways of living is enlightening. Let me give you a personal example. When I was growing up, my family and I lived in China for a couple years. Many aspects of the culture, such as eating, were very different from those in my home country. Unlike in my home country, people in China are encouraged to share food. So while we were in China, we adopted their eating practices and shared our food with one another. It was foreign to us, but we decided to follow Chinese customs so long as we were living there.

Another reason to adopt new customs is that doing so allows you to fit more easily into the local community. People who refuse to adopt their new nation's customs are never able to integrate into the larger society. However, by following local customs, you are able to make more friends with the local people and become a part of their group. When my wife and I moved to Germany, we were eager to take part in some German festivals. One of these was Oktoberfest. We went with our neighbors to the city market for the celebration. We ate great food, played games, and had a lot of fun. More importantly, we made great friends. This made us feel like welcomed members of the community.

Moving to a new country is an opportunity to live an entirely different life. Although some people may prefer to cling to their old ways, for the reasons given above, I think it is much better to adopt local customs.

| Critical Analysis | Refer to the sample response to complete the tasks below.

**1** Underline the topic sentence in each paragraph.

**2** Double underline the sentences that include supporting details.

**3** List at least two of the examples the writer uses on the lines below.

_____

_____

_____

Moving to a new country is exciting. But it can also be stress full. Some people miss the things from their home country. And for good reasons. Therefore, I think it is better to follow the customs from the old country instead of adopt the new country customs.

First of all, keeping the old customs makes like easy in the new country. You have to know about your way of live, so keeping the old customs can make this more comfortable. Like when you have to eat. Do you want to eat the new food from the country? Maybe some times it is ok to try. But most of time, people would perfer the food from old country. Like my friend Muhammad. His family comes from Iran. They only cook food from Iran in their house. This is because they eated it for, such a long time. It is what they used to. In this way, keeping old customs is better for most people.

Next, people can not simple giving up their old customs. They have to keep with their ways for some time. I mean, think about it. If you are always living at a certian way, how can you just stop living in that way? The answer is, you can't. For instance, if you moving to a different country, the language, culture, way of life is all different. You can't just stop living your old way and become integrated into the new place right away. It take some time. Maybe, after some time, it is possible to join the new community. But for a while, you have to keep your old customs.

Moving to a new country is exciting. However, it also has its problem. When you move to a new country, it is more easy to keep your old customs. at least for a while.

---

**| Critical Analysis |**   Refer to the sample response to complete the tasks below.

**1**   Where could the following sentence be added to strengthen the response?

**For example, his family does not eat pork products because it goes against their religion.**

   Ⓐ  Body paragraph 1

   Ⓑ  Body paragraph 2

   Ⓒ  Final paragraph

**2**   The topic sentence from the second body paragraph is not clear. Rewrite it to make it clearer.

**3**   Think of at least one supporting idea to add to the second body paragraph to make it more interesting.

**4**   Find at least two grammatical mistakes in the response. Write the corrected sentences on the lines below.

# Part **B**

# Anthropology: **The Purpose of Ancient Roads**

🔊 **Vocabulary** Take a few moments to review the vocabulary items that will appear in this task.

**fascinating** *adj.* pleasing to the eye or mind
I love listening to my grandfather's stories. They are so **fascinating**.

**ancient** *adj.* very old; lasting a long time
When we went to the desert, we found some **ancient** dinosaur bones.

**archaeologist** *n.* a scientist who studies past cultures and people
My mother is an **archaeologist**, so she gets to work in many faraway places.

**transportation** *n.* the act of moving people or things around
Most large cities have a **transportation** system that includes buses, subways, and taxis.

**stretch** *v.* to reach; to extend
If you **stretch** your arm, you should just be able to reach the top shelf.

**accommodate** *v.* to hold comfortably without crowding
Our hotel can **accommodate** 400 guests.

**significance** *n.* having importance or a special meaning
Although it may look like an ordinary watch, it actually holds great **significance** for me.

**honor** *v.* to show respect toward
I am so **honored** to win this award.

**mound** *n.* a pile of earth, gravel, sand, or rocks
In old times, the Chinese people would bury their dead under large dirt **mounds**.

**constellation** *n.* a group of stars that appears to form an image in the sky
There are 88 **constellations** that can be seen from the Earth. The most famous one is the Big Dipper.

## Reading

Read the passage carefully. Try to understand what the main argument of the passage is. You have 3 minutes to read.

The Native Americans of North America left many fascinating artifacts from their early history. Among the most mysterious are the enormous ancient roads they constructed. The exact purpose of these roads remains unknown, but several compelling theories have been put forth to explain their existence.

The most commonly argued theory is that the roads were used for transportation. Many of these ancient roads stretch for several miles across different regions. These roads were built using the most advanced technology of their time and were very wide and straight. Therefore, they could have easily accommodated a large number of travelers going between different towns. There is also evidence to suggest that these roads were used to transport crops from fields to nearby villages.

Another popular theory is that the roads were constructed for religious purposes. Archaeologists believe that the shapes and the locations of these roads were of great religious significance. They contend that many roads were built to honor a god or to celebrate a religious figure. For example, the Great Hopewell Road in central Ohio runs alongside a river for more than fifty miles. At the beginning and the end of the road are two large circular mounds. Together, the road and the mounds form a shape similar to that of a constellation that was important to the Native American tribe that made the road. Based on these findings, it is safe to conclude that these ancient roads held tremendous religious importance.

___

**| Paraphrasing |** The following sentences come from the reading passage. Complete each paraphrase with appropriate words or phrases.

1   The exact purpose of these roads remains unknown, but several compelling theories have been put forth to explain their existence.

→ *Although archaeologists do not know what the roads* _____ *, they have several ideas.*

2   Therefore, they could have easily accommodated a large number of travelers going between different towns.

→ *Thus, it is possible that these roads allowed* _____ *to* _____ .

3   Archaeologists believe that the shapes and the locations of these roads were of great religious significance.

→ *Researchers contend that these roads were of religious significance based on* _____ .

4   Based on these findings, it is safe to conclude that these ancient roads held tremendous religious importance.

→ *From this research, we can understand the* _____ *of these* _____ .

**| Summarizing |** Complete the summary below by using the information from the reading passage. Be sure to paraphrase the information.

In the reading passage, the purpose of _____ is discussed. There are two supporting arguments. The first is that roads were used _____ . This is based on the fact that the roads were _____ , meaning that they could have accommodated a large number of people. The second issue discussed is _____ of the roads. According to the passage, _____ of the roads were of great religious significance.

## Vocabulary Take a few moments to review the vocabulary items that will appear in this task.

**put forth** *phr v.* to suggest something

At the meeting, she **put forth** the idea that employees should get longer lunch breaks.

**solely** *adv.* only; entirely

It is **solely** up to you to complete the job.

**unnecessarily** *adv.* possible to do without; not needed

Please do not speak **unnecessarily** while the teacher is talking.

**vehicle** *n.* a machine that is used for transporting people or goods

Cars, trucks, and buses are **vehicles** that people use to get around in.

**means** *n.* how a result is obtained or an end is achieved

You must use any **means** necessary to get the money.

**seldom** *adv.* not often; infrequently; rarely

I used to go to the park every day, but now I **seldom** go there.

**highway** *n.* a main road that usually connects different cities

**Highway** 66 runs from Chicago to Los Angeles.

**artifact** *n.* an object made by human beings, especially a tool or weapon of archaeological interest

The people from this area left many **artifacts**, including tools, bowls, and weapons.

## Listening

Now listen to part of a lecture on the topic you just read about.

02-05

| **Paraphrasing** | The following sentences come from the lecture. Complete each paraphrase with appropriate words or phrases.

**1** Well, the fact is that these roads were simply too large to have been used just to move people and things.

→ *The roads could not have been used* _____ *because they were*

_____ .

**2** People rarely traveled more than a few miles from their homes during their lifetimes.

→ *Most people did not* _____ *over the course* _____ .

**3** The majority of these ancient roads have been completely destroyed by centuries of farming and development, so it is impossible to determine the exact layout of these roads.

→ *It is not possible to know* _____ *due to all* _____

*that has occurred over the years.*

**4** Many artifacts from these cultures have been lost, so we don't know what religion these people had or even if they were religious at all.

→ *Because few* _____ *still exist, it is not possible to determine whether these*

*people* _____ .

| **Summarizing** | Complete the summary below by using the information from the lecture. Be sure to paraphrase the information.

In the lecture, the professor explains that the purpose of the Native American roads remains unknown. His first argument is that the roads _____ to be used only for transportation. He adds that most people at that time _____ and rarely went far from their homes. His next point relates to _____ of the roads. The instructor states that most of the roads have been destroyed over the years, so it is impossible to know _____ . Furthermore, he contends that there are not enough _____ to know if they even had religion.

Refer to the paraphrasing and summarizing exercises to complete the side-by-side notes below. Include only the two points from the reading and the listening that clearly contract each other.

| READING | LISTENING |
|---|---|
| **Main Idea** | **Main Idea** |
| *Many compelling ideas have been put forth* | *There is not enough evidence to determine* |
| *to* | |
| | |
| **First Supporting Argument** | **First Supporting Argument** |
| *One theory is that these roads were used for* | *The roads were too large to be used only for* |
| | |
| Supporting Detail | Supporting Detail |
| | |
| **Second Supporting Argument** | **Second Supporting Argument** |
| *The roads were of great* | *There is no evidence to suggest that* |
| | |
| Supporting Detail | Supporting Detail |
| | |

## Writing

Use this page to write your response. You have 20 minutes to complete your essay.

| Writing Guide | Summarize the points made in the lecture, being sure to explain how they challenge specific claims made in the reading passage. |
|---|---|
| **First Paragraph** ◌<br><br>State and discuss thesis<br><br>**Second Paragraph** ◌<br><br>First main idea from lecture<br><br>Contradiction from reading<br><br>Supporting detail<br><br>**Third Paragraph** ◌<br><br>Second main idea from lecture<br><br>Contradiction from reading<br><br>Supporting detail<br><br>**Fourth Paragraph** ◌<br><br>Conclusion (optional) | |

🔖 **Scaffolding**    Here are some useful phrases to help you when you write.

> In the reading passage, it is argued that…

> In the lecture, however, the professor contradicts…

> To begin with, the instructor doubts that…

> On top of this, the roads were…

> His arguments refute the reading passage's assertion that…

> The lecturer's second point deals with…

> In this way, the instructor rebuts the reading passage's claim that…

In the reading passage, it is argued that ancient Native Americans built large roads for transportation and religious purposes. In the lecture, however, the professor contradicts these assumptions.

The instructor starts his lecture by expressing his doubts that the roads were used for transportation. He explains that because the roads were so wide, they could not have been used only for this purpose. The professor adds that there were no vehicles at the time, so people were not able to travel very far anyway. His arguments refute the reading passage's assertion that these ancient roads were built to accommodate a large number of people traveling between villages.

The lecturer goes on to question the theory that the roads were built for religious purposes. He explains that there is no evidence to support this idea because the roads have been destroyed by many years of development. He further states that few artifacts from these ancient cultures still exist, so archaeologists are not sure whether these ancient people even had any religious beliefs. In this way, the instructor rebuts the reading passage's claim that the shapes and the locations of these roads were of great religious significance.

| Critical Analysis |   Refer to the sample response to complete the tasks below.

1   Underline the topic sentence in each paragraph.

2   Double underline the sentences that refer to the listening.

3   Which word in the response means "**having importance**"? Write the word on the line below.

_____

4   What does "**accommodate**" mean? Find the sentence that explains this and write it on the lines below.

_____

_____

5   List at least two of the transitions the writer uses on the lines below.

_____

_____

_____

The passages mainly about ancient roads. Reading said ancient roads had many purpose. The listening said the roads are not sure about why built.

First of all the reading, state the roads were build many times ago, by the Ancient Americans for transport. The roads, were transport for used, across many different regions. Since they were very straight, the letted people go between villages. **1** The reading also continued that roads were for religious purposes. This is their significant. **2** For example the road in Ohio runs for more than 50 miles. **3** These findings show how significances their were.

Second of all, the lecture said the roads could have not be, for these reasons. For instance, people only walked to their travelling, so the roads, weren't not need. Also, the long highways were just too large for the people and the things. Then the lecture said that land has changed a lot. therefore the proof, has not been found. In this way, the lecture dis prove the theories, in the reading.

---

**| Critical Analysis |**   Refer to the sample response to complete the tasks below.

**1**   In which of the following ways should the highlighted sentence be rewritten?

    (A) According to the reading passage, Native Americans rebuilt their roads many times.

    (B) The reading passage begins by arguing that these roads are more ancient than was previously thought.

    (C) The first part of the reading passage states that these ancient roads were used for transportation.

**2**   Where should the following sentence be added to improve the response?

**The shape of this road is similar to a constellation of great religious importance to the tribe that built it.**

    (A) **1**

    (B) **2**

    (C) **3**

**3**   Find at least two grammatical mistakes in the response. Write the corrected sentences on the lines below.

_____

_____

_____

# Meeting the Needs of Others to Be Happy

 Do you agree or disagree with the following statement? People are happier when they meet the needs of others rather than their own needs. Use specific reasons and examples to support your answer.

## Generating Ideas

The following questions will help you write your response. Answer each with one or two sentences. Plan an answer for both options. Some ideas have been provided to help you.

### Idea Box   Agree

**1 Q** Why do people like to help others?

**A** *People like to improve other people's lives. They also like the way they feel after helping others.*

**2 Q** How can people help others in need?

**A** *They can*

**3 Q** How do people often feel after they help others in need?

**A** *People often feel*

Reason 1:

Reason 2:

### Idea Box   Disagree

**1 Q** Why do some people prefer taking care of their own needs than the needs of others?

**A** *They want to improve their lives and feel good at the same time.*

**2 Q** What might make people not want to help others?

**A** *Some people are*

**3 Q** How can helping oneself be beneficial?

**A** *It can*

Reason 1:

Reason 2:

## Developing Ideas

Having examined the two options, which do you feel more comfortable developing into an essay? Explain why you feel this way.

Use the outline to plan your response to the following: Do you agree or disagree with the following statement? People are happier when they meet the needs of others rather than their own needs. Use specific reasons and examples to support your answer.

| Agree | Disagree |
|---|---|
| **Thesis Statement** | **Thesis Statement** |
| *I think that people are definitely happier when they meet others' needs rather than their own.* | *I believe people become happier when they take care of themselves.* |
| **First Supporting Idea** | **First Supporting Idea** |
| | |
| Supporting Example | Supporting Example |
| | |
| **Second Supporting Idea** | **Second Supporting Idea** |
| | |
| Supporting Example | Supporting Example |
| | |
| **Conclusion** | **Conclusion** |
| | |

## Writing

Use this page to write your response. You have 30 minutes to complete your essay.

| Writing Guide | Do you agree or disagree with the following statement? People are happier when they meet the needs of others rather than their own needs. Use specific reasons and examples to support your answer. |
|---|---|
| **First Paragraph** ○<br><br>State and discuss thesis | |
| **Second Paragraph** ○<br><br>First main supporting idea<br><br>Supporting detail<br><br>Example | |
| **Third Paragraph** ○<br><br>Second main supporting idea<br><br>Supporting detail<br><br>Example | |
| **Fourth Paragraph** ○<br><br>Conclusion | |

**Scaffolding**   Here are some useful phrases to help you when you write.

> While some people become happier when they…

> First, more people become happier when…

> Second, plenty of people have…

> For starters, when people… they become…

> I have never seen…

> People are always happier when they…

> Furthermore, there are a large number of people who…

> Although a few people… the majority…

While some people become happier when they meet the needs of others rather than their own needs, I strongly disagree with this statement. First, more people become happier when taking care of themselves. Second, plenty of people have no interest in taking care of the needs of others.

For starters, when people look after their own needs, they become very happy. For example, my uncle just bought a brand-new car a few days ago. He drove his car to my family's house to show it to us yesterday. He was so proud of his car and looked extremely happy as he was talking about it. I could easily tell that he was happy after buying that car. His previous car was old and broke down frequently. So he took care of his own needs by acquiring a new vehicle. I have never seen someone take care of another person's needs and look as happy as my uncle did yesterday. There is simply no comparison between the two. I have seen many other examples of people feeling happy by taking care of their own needs, even for small things. People are always happier when they look after themselves and their needs first.

Furthermore, there are a large number of people who lack interest in taking care of other people's needs. Last month, my school had a fundraiser. The school needed money to improve its facilities. Many students visited local residents to tell them about the event. I was one of those students. Although a few people were willing to donate, the majority were not interested even in giving a small amount of money. Some of them were actually quite rude about it. Clearly, those people do not care about helping others. So they would definitely be happier helping themselves since they do not bother to assist others.

People are not happier when helping others rather than themselves. Instead, the opposite happens, and lots of people do not help others in any way.

| **Critical Analysis** | Refer to the sample response to complete the tasks below.

1    Underline the topic sentence in each paragraph.

2    Double underline the sentences that include supporting details.

3    List at least two of the examples the writer uses on the lines below.

_____

_____

_____

Lots of people enjoy help out others. In fact, these people frequently prefer to assisting others before they help themselves. They feel good about themselves after they help others with problems. In addition, there are many unselfish people. They are interested in helping others instead of helping themselves. I therefore agreeing with the statement. I believe that people are happier when they meet the needs of others rather than their own needs.

To beginning with, there are many people who feel good when they help the others with problems. My brother is one of this kind of people. If a friend has a problem, he will always offer assistance. The other days, a friend called my brother and ask for help. My brother had to study for a test at school the next day. But he stopped studying and immediately went to help his friend. When my brother returned back home it was too late for him to study. The tomorrow, he did poorly on his test. But he did not care about that so much. He was proud helping his friend even though it wound up hurt him.

Another reason I agree with the statement is that many unselfish people are there a lot. These people are extremely focused on helping others. They would prefer help others than to help themselves. My teachers be an unselfish person. She is always willing to help the students in her classes. She stays lately at school almost everyday because she is trying to get her students to improve themselves. She does not worry about her own. My teacher says that she is happy when she knows what she is making students' lives better.

People are not always happiest when they take care of their ownselves needs. Instead, they are usually happier when they look after the needs of others. There are also many unselfish people who are interested in improves the lives of other people. For those two reasons, I am agreeing with the statement.

---

| **Critical Analysis** |   Refer to the sample response to complete the tasks below.

1   Which of the following sentences could be added to strengthen the response?
   (A) I wish that more people would take care of themselves instead of looking after others.
   (B) There are many people who dedicate their lives to solving problems that other people have.
   (C) People have lots of work to do, so they ought to focus on doing that work at once.

2   The topic sentence from the second body paragraph is not clear. Rewrite it to make it clearer.

3   Think of at least one supporting idea to add to the second body paragraph to make it more interesting.

4   Find at least two grammatical mistakes in the response. Write the corrected sentences on the lines below.

# Part **B**

**Chapter 06**

# Botany: **Preventing Mimosa Trees from Growing Too Much**

**Q Vocabulary** Take a few moments to review the vocabulary items that will appear in this task.

**ornamental** *adj.* decorative; used as a decoration

Most **ornamental** plants look good but serve no other purpose.

**invasive species** *n.* any species that is not native to the area in which it is living

That insect is an **invasive species** which is harming many native plants.

**tendency** *n.* a natural inclination or leaning to act in a certain way

She has a **tendency** to wake up early in the morning and then go jogging.

**crowd out** *phr v.* to push or force someone or something out of an area

These flowers are **crowding out** the other plants in the garden.

**pod** *n.* a long case in which there are seeds

When he opened the **pod**, several seeds fell out.

**dangle** *v.* to hang loosely, often while swinging back and forth

The hiker is **dangling** from the rope and is in danger.

**gather** *v.* to collect

He often goes into the forest and **gathers** wild mushrooms.

**strip** *n.* a long, thin piece of something

She tore off **strips** of cloth and then tied them together.

**bark** *n.* the hard outer covering of a tree trunk

The thick **bark** of this tree protects it when there are forest fires.

**soil** *n.* dirt; earth; ground

The **soil** in this part of the country is ideal for growing cotton.

## Reading

Read the passage carefully. Try to understand what the main argument of the passage is. You have 3 minutes to read.

One popular ornamental tree is the mimosa. It is easy to take care of, grows well in heat, does not require much water, and looks wonderful. Some people, however, consider it an invasive species because it has a tendency to take over people's yards. New mimosa trees can grow swiftly and crowd out other types of vegetation. Fortunately, there are ways to prevent mimosas from growing too much in a yard or garden.

The best way to be sure that the number of mimosas growing in an area is low is to prevent seeds from getting into the soil. The mimosa produces seed pods that dangle from the tree. A gardener can simply collect the seed pods from the tree itself or wait until they fall to the ground to gather them. If a person is careful enough to collect all of the seeds, then new, unwanted mimosa trees will be unable to grow.

A second way to remove mimosa trees is to physically destroy them. This can be accomplished in a couple of ways. The first way is just to cut the trees down at the ground level. This can remove undesired growth. A second way is to engage in something called girdling. Girdling involves cutting a strip of bark off all around the tree around fifteen centimeters above the soil. If the cut is made deep enough, then the upper part of the tree will die. The gardener can then remove the tree at any time.

**| Paraphrasing |** The following sentences come from the reading passage. Complete each paraphrase with appropriate words or phrases.

1  Some people, however, consider it an invasive species because it has a tendency to take over people's yards.

→ *It is* _____ *because it can take over* _____ .

2  New mimosa trees can grow swiftly and crowd out other types of vegetation.

→ *The mimosa* _____ *and can* _____ .

3  A gardener can simply collect the seed pods from the tree itself or wait until they fall to the ground to gather them.

→ *A gardener can* _____ *or pick them up after they*

_____ .

4  If the cut is made deep enough, then the upper part of the tree will die.

→ *By* _____ *enough into the tree,* _____ *will die.*


**| Summarizing |** Complete the summary below by using the information from the reading passage. Be sure to paraphrase the information.

The mimosa tree is _____ that can take over people's yards. It is hard to

_____ once it starts growing. The mimosa tree _____ that a

person can take from a tree or pick up off the ground. That can keep trees from growing. A person can also

_____ at the ground level or use girdling by _____ . Either

method will make the trees die.

## Vocabulary  Take a few moments to review the vocabulary items that will appear in this task.

**particularly** *adv.* especially; very

The sun is **particularly** bright at this time of day.

**attractive** *adj.* good looking; beautiful

She thinks that gold necklace is very **attractive**.

**get rid of** *phr v.* to remove; to eliminate

It can be very hard to **get rid of** some weeds in a vegetable garden.

**viable** *adj.* capable of living

This plant is still **viable**, so put it in a pot and give it water.

**ideal** *adj.* perfect; very good

Tomorrow night is the **ideal** time for everyone to meet.

**germinate** *v.* to start to grow or develop

Once the seed **germinates**, it will develop roots and then grow a stem.

**monumental** *adv.* enormous; huge; very large

This is a **monumental** problem, but we can solve it by working together.

**task** *n.* a job; a chore; work to be done

Please finish all of your **tasks** before the sun goes down.

**resprout** *v.* to start growing again

Many plants will **resprout** if they still have roots in the soil.

**take over** *phr v.* to take control over; to control completely

The army plans to **take over** the entire region in order to control it.

## Listening

Now listen to part of a lecture on the topic you just read about.

02-06

**| Paraphrasing |**  The following sentences come from the lecture. Complete each paraphrase with appropriate words or phrases.

**1**  Unfortunately, once mimosa trees start growing, they're almost impossible to get rid of.

→ *It is* _____ *to get rid of mimosa trees in places where they are growing.*

**2**  You should also know that mimosa seeds can remain viable in the soil for several years and not grow if conditions aren't ideal.

→ *It is possible for mimosa seeds to* _____ *for years without growing until*
_____ .

**3**  You see, trying to get rid of the seeds is a monumental task.

→ *Getting rid of the seeds is* _____ .

**4**  This means that if the roots remain in the ground, new trees can grow even after the original tree has died.

→ *As long as* _____ *, new trees can* _____ *even if the original tree is gone.*

**| Summarizing |**  Complete the summary below by using the information from the lecture. Be sure to paraphrase the information.

In the lecture, the professor points out that the suggested ways of _____ have problems. She mentions that mimosa trees produce _____ . Getting all of them will be hard. The seeds can also grow years after they have fallen into the soil and may also be _____ . The problem with cutting down the trees and girdling is that _____ . New trees can resprout from the roots. _____ is possible, but that is too much work for most people.

## Tandem Note-Taking

Refer to the paraphrasing and summarizing exercises to complete the side-by-side notes below. Include only the two points from the reading and the listening that clearly contract each other.

### READING

**Main Idea**

*It is possible to prevent mimosa trees*

**First Supporting Argument**

*A person can prevent seed pods*

Supporting Detail

**Second Supporting Argument**

*A person can*

Supporting Detail

### LISTENING

**Main Idea**

*The suggested methods of getting rid of mimosa trees*

**First Supporting Argument**

*It is nearly impossible to*

Supporting Detail

**Second Supporting Argument**

*New trees can*

Supporting Detail

Use this page to write your response. You have 20 minutes to complete your essay.

| Writing Guide | Summarize the points made in the lecture, being sure to explain how they cast doubt on specific arguments made in the reading passage. |
|---|---|
| **First Paragraph** ○<br><br>State and discuss thesis | |
| **Second Paragraph** ○<br><br>First main idea from lecture<br><br>Contradiction from reading<br><br>Supporting detail | |
| **Third Paragraph** ○<br><br>Second main idea from lecture<br><br>Contradiction from reading<br><br>Supporting detail | |
| **Fourth Paragraph** ○<br><br>Conclusion (optional) | |

**Scaffolding**    Here are some useful phrases to help you when you write.

- The reading passage and the lecture discuss…
- The reading passage claims that…
- However, the professor counters by stating that…
- The professor points out that…

- In this way, the professor casts doubt on…
- The professor also argues that…
- She therefore goes against the argument in the reading passage that…

The reading passage and the lecture discuss removing unwanted mimosa trees. The reading passage claims that it is possible to prevent mimosa trees from growing in certain areas. However, the professor counters by stating that the suggested solutions all have problems.

The professor points out that mimosa trees grow thousands of seeds. Collecting every seed would be difficult. In addition, the seeds can germinate after several years of being in the ground and be spread by animals. In this way, the professor casts doubt on the solution in the reading passage that every seed can be removed to prevent new trees from growing.

The professor also argues that mimosa trees can resprout from roots that remain in the ground. She claims that the only way to get rid of them is to dig up the roots. But this is too much work for most people. She therefore goes against the argument in the reading passage that cutting down trees and using girdling can remove undesired mimosa trees.

| Critical Analysis | Refer to the sample response to complete the tasks below.

1 Underline the topic sentence in each paragraph.

2 Double underline the sentences that refer to the listening.

3 Which word in the response means "**gathering**"? Write the word on the line below.

_____

4 What does "**prevent**" mean? Find the sentence that explains this and write it on the lines below.

_____

_____

5 List at least two of the transitions the writer uses on the lines below.

_____

_____

_____

The reading claim you can remove mimosa trees. The lecture say no you can not do. The professor say are problems removing mimosa trees.

The professor she say one tree makes thousands of seeds every year. So can not pick up all seeds. Some seeds stay in the ground for years. Then grow later. The reading passage says it's okay. You can get seeds from trees or from the ground.

Next, the professor mention mimosa tree can grow again. It is resprout. If there are roots in the ground, then more trees grow. **1** You need to get roots. **2** This is against the reading passage. **3** It claims is okay to cut down trees or removing bark.

The professor thinks the reading is wrong. She says is too hard to get rid of mimosa trees.

| Critical Analysis | Refer to the sample response to complete the tasks below.

1   In which of the following ways should the highlighted sentence be rewritten?

    (A) The professor first argues that a single tree can produce thousands of seeds annually.

    (B) The professor's first argument is that thousands of mimosa trees grow every year.

    (C) The first problem the professor talks about is the fact that some mimosa trees make no seeds.

2   Where should the following sentence be added to improve the response?

**However, digging them up is often too difficult for most people to do.**

    (A) **1**

    (B) **2**

    (C) **3**

3   Find at least two grammatical mistakes in the response. Write the corrected sentences on the lines below.

_____

_____

_____

# Governments Should Focus on Health Care

Do you agree or disagree with the following statement? Governments should pay more attention to healthcare issues than environmental issues. Use specific reasons and examples to support your answer.

## Generating Ideas

The following questions will help you write your response. Answer each with one or two sentences. Plan an answer for both options. Some ideas have been provided to help you.

### Idea Box    Agree

**1 Q** How can free government healthcare benefit an entire nation?

**A** *When more people are healthy, more work can be done, and more money can be spent.*

**2 Q** What obligations do governments have to their people?

**A** *Governments should*

**3 Q** How are healthcare problems easier to fix than environmental issues?

**A** *They are easier to fix in that*

Reason 1:

Reason 2:

### Idea Box    Disagree

**1 Q** How do environmental problems affect every person in a nation?

**A** *Only some people need health care, but everybody has to live with the environment.*

**2 Q** In what ways can the environment affect other issues, such as health care?

**A** *The environment can*

**3 Q** How are environmental problems easier to fix than healthcare issues?

**A** *They are easier to fix in that*

Reason 1:

Reason 2:

## Developing Ideas

Having examined the two options, which do you feel more comfortable developing into an essay? Explain why you feel this way.

Use the outline to plan your response to the following: Do you agree or disagree with the following statement? Governments should pay more attention to healthcare issues than environmental issues. Use specific reasons and examples to support your answer.

| Agree | Disagree |
|---|---|
| **Thesis Statement** | **Thesis Statement** |
| *I contend that governments must make health care their most important issue.* | *While health care is important, I believe that nations must focus more on the environment.* |
| **First Supporting Idea** | **First Supporting Idea** |
| | |
| Supporting Example | Supporting Example |
| | |
| **Second Supporting Idea** | **Second Supporting Idea** |
| | |
| Supporting Example | Supporting Example |
| | |
| **Conclusion** | **Conclusion** |
| | |

Use this page to write your response. You have 30 minutes to complete your essay.

| Writing Guide | Do you agree or disagree with the following statement? Governments should pay more attention to healthcare issues than environmental issues. Use specific reasons and examples to support your answer. |
|---|---|

**First Paragraph** ○

State and discuss thesis

**Second Paragraph** ○

First main supporting idea

Supporting detail

Example

**Third Paragraph** ○

Second main supporting idea

Supporting detail

Example

**Fourth Paragraph** ○

Conclusion

**Scaffolding**   Here are some useful phrases to help you when you write.

➤ As important as this issue is, I feel that…

➤ Therefore, it is clear that governments need to…

➤ Health care is something that everybody…

➤ The environment is the one thing that…

➤ For example, consider…

➤ On top of this, addressing… can help…

➤ As a result of… thousands of people…

➤ Ultimately, I contend that…

These days, the world is filled with many problems. For a lot of people, receiving adequate health care is a great concern. As important as this issue is, however, there is one issue of even greater importance: the environment. Our future depends on how well we take care of the Earth. Therefore, it is clear that governments around the world need to make environmental issues their top priority.

The environment is the one thing that affects everyone in the world. It is terrible if a father cannot support his family because he does not have health care. But this only affects a small number of people. The fact of the matter is that if the Earth suffers, then all of humanity suffers. This is evident in a number of problems we are currently facing. For example, consider the main resource that we all take for granted: water. Clean water supplies all over the world are running out. This is happening for a variety of reasons. They include pollution by companies and overuse by individuals. As serious as the water problem is, it can still be corrected but only if governments make an effort to protect the environment.

On top of this, addressing environmental issues can help solve other problems and prevent them from occurring in the future. The reason is that many of the world's problems, including the spread of diseases, are results of environmental issues. Think about how the environment can affect a person's health. In developing nations such as China, the air is polluted due to smog from factories and automobiles. As a result of this pollution, thousands of people develop health problems and have to go to the hospital each year. Virtually all of these cases could be prevented if the Chinese government made stricter regulations concerning air pollution. Because the environment affects everything, governments could solve countless problems by addressing environmental concerns.

Although governments around the world have many serious issues to tackle, I believe that they should make environmental issues their top priority. By protecting the environment, governments will be able to improve all other aspects of their citizens' lives.

| **Critical Analysis** | Refer to the sample response to complete the tasks below.

1  Underline the topic sentence in each paragraph.

2  Double underline the sentences that include supporting details.

3  List at least two of the examples the writer uses on the lines below.

_____

_____

_____

Today there is a lot of debate about the health care and the environment. It seems that people must worry alot about both. The environment is not as important as the health care.

In the beginning staying healthy is important, when you are healthy you can do more, but not healthy cant do any thing. But if the health care is too cost then, people cant stay health, so the government, has to make health care more avalable. Therefore, the health care is more importent then, the environment.

Further more, most people can not have health alone. They have to get the nation to assist, other wise they have no health. This is called insurance, insurance is very important to stay health, but for most it can cost to expensive. Therefore, the government has to make health care for every body.

Finally, fixing the environment is a big problem. It will take a long time to fix. Since it will take a lot tie, we have to look at the other problem first, since health care is so a problem, it will need to be fix first. The government can spend less money to have health people than the environment. In this way, it becomes logical to fix the health care before hand.

Although environment is a serious problem, it does not have the importance, health care has. So the government needs to look at it first.

---

**| Critical Analysis |**   Refer to the sample response to complete the tasks below.

**1**   Which of the following sentences could be added to strengthen the response?

   Ⓐ  According to recent surveys, a majority of people view environmental issues as the most important.

   Ⓑ  To give a personal example, my father was able to get health insurance from his employer.

   Ⓒ  One estimate suggests that developing cheap alternative energy sources will take thirty more years.

**2**   The topic sentence from the second body paragraph is not clear. Rewrite it to make it clearer.

**3**   Think of at least one supporting idea to add to the first body paragraph to make it more interesting.

**4**   Find at least two grammatical mistakes in the response. Write the corrected sentences on the lines below.

# Part **B**

# Business: **Paying Employees on Commission**

## ◯ **Vocabulary**   Take a few moments to review the vocabulary items that will appear in this task.

**boost**  *v.* to make higher or greater; to increase

To make the city safer, the mayor wants to **boost** the number of police officers on the streets.

**productivity**  *n.* the amount of work a person does

My **productivity** is at its highest during the early afternoon.

**efficiency**  *n.* the amount of work needed to produce something

Cars with greater fuel **efficiency** can go farther while using less gas.

**incentive**  *n.* something that causes a person to act in a certain way

Offering candy is a good **incentive** to get children to do their chores.

**staff**  *n.* workers; employees

There are twenty people on the **staff** at the bank.

**flat**  *adj.* unchanging; fixed

Some lawmakers have put forth the idea of having a **flat** tax rate.

**factor**  *n.* a cause that brings about a result

There are many **factors** to think about when choosing a job.

**attractive**  *adj.* having the power to please or draw interest

Although both women are pretty, I think Mia is the more **attractive** of the two.

**reward**  *v.* to give something in return, especially for good work or a good deed

Brent was **rewarded** 50,000 dollars for helping police catch the criminal.

**cycle**  *n.* a set of events that keep coming back in the same order

The weather goes through the same **cycle** each year.

## Reading

Read the passage carefully. Try to understand what the main argument of the passage is. You have 3 minutes to read.

Companies around the world all want to boost the productivity and work efficiency of their employees. In order to do this, employers must be willing to offer their employees incentives to work harder. One of the best incentives is money. It is for this reason that employers should get rid of traditional salaries in favor of paying their staff on commission.

Paying employees on commission greatly benefits companies. Workers who are paid based on their overall productivity generally work much more efficiently than those paid flat salaries. This was the case at one company that decided to pay its employees on commission. It found that the workers completed their work thirty percent faster than when they had received salaries. Furthermore, these employees also tended to do work of a higher quality. These two factors make commission-based payments an attractive option for employers.

Employees also benefit from being paid on commission. When paid based on the amount of work they do, employees are able to double or even triple their previous salaries. Earning more money allows workers to enjoy a higher quality of life. In addition, employees who work on commission have increased job satisfaction because they know their hard work will be properly rewarded. This satisfaction at work makes employees happier and healthier in general. In turn, employees are able to work with greater efficiency, allowing them to earn more money and enjoy even greater job satisfaction.

| Paraphrasing | The following sentences come from the reading passage. Complete each paraphrase with appropriate words or phrases.

1   Workers who are paid based on their overall productivity generally work much more efficiently than those paid flat salaries.

→ *When paid for the amount of work* _____ *, employees tend to work*

_____ .

2   It found that the workers completed their work thirty percent faster than when they had received salaries.

→ *Employees paid on commission finish their tasks* _____ *compared to*

*employees* _____ .

3   When paid based on the amount of work they do, employees are able to double or even triple their previous salaries.

→ *Workers paid on commission can earn* _____ *their original salaries.*

4   In addition, employees who work on commission have increased job satisfaction because they know their hard work will be properly rewarded.

→ *People who are paid for the amount of work they do are* _____ *since their*

_____ .

| Summarizing | Complete the summary below by using the information from the reading passage. Be sure to paraphrase the information.

The author of the reading passage contends that _____ benefits both

_____ . It benefits employers in that workers become _____ .

On top of this, employees paid on commission do work of _____ . At the same time,

receiving a commission is good for employees because they are able to _____ . Not

only does this allow them to enjoy a higher quality of life, but it also gives workers

_____ .

## 🎧 Vocabulary  Take a few moments to review the vocabulary items that will appear in this task.

**forgo**  *v.* to do without; to let go of something

If you want to camp in the woods, you will have to **forgo** some of the comforts of home.

**steady**  *adj.* unchanging

The price of food has remained **steady** even though everything else has become more expensive.

**skeptical**  *adj.* having or showing doubt; disbelieving

Some people believe in ghosts, but I am **skeptical** myself.

**suited**  *adj.* meant or adapted for an occasion or use; appropriate

That flashlight is **suited** for underwater use.

**assume**  *v.* to take for granted; to suppose

Try not to **assume** too many things. If you do, you may get in trouble.

**guarantee**  *v.* to make certain

The computer comes with a free ninety-day **guarantee**.

**fluctuate**  *v.* to rise and fall; to change continually

Temperatures have been **fluctuating** lately. One day, it is freezing, but the next day, it is hot.

**virtually**  *adv.* almost but not quite; nearly; practically

**Virtually** everybody learns how to read by the time they are ten years old.

**contract**  *n.* an agreement, particularly one that is written

Before you start the job, you must sign the **contract** first.

**stability**  *n.* the state of being unchanging

Most people want **stability** in their lives, but some people like for each day to be different.

## Listening

Now listen to part of a lecture on the topic you just read about.

02-07

| **Paraphrasing** | The following sentences come from the lecture. Complete each paraphrase with appropriate words or phrases.

**1** Of course, some jobs are well suited to commission-based payments.

→ *There are certain* _____ *that should be* _____ .

**2** Every student would always pass every class.

→ *No students would ever fail* _____ .

**3** Paying employees on commission does not always guarantee an increase in salary.

→ *Workers who are paid for the number of* _____ *do not always*

_____ .

**4** This lack of stability can make employees uncomfortable with their financial situations, and this can greatly reduce their work productivity.

→ *People who do not have* _____ *can become nervous about*

_____ , *which makes them unable to* _____ .

| **Summarizing** | Complete the summary below by using the information from the lecture. Be sure to paraphrase the information.

The instructor opposes paying _____ . He gives two arguments in favor of his opinion. First, the professor explains that not all jobs should be paid on commission. To illustrate this, he uses the example of teachers. He says that teachers would benefit from _____ , but students would not. Next, the lecturer talks about how being paid for the amount of work done does not always _____ in salary. He clarifies this by talking about how _____ a person earns _____ from month to month.

Refer to the paraphrasing and summarizing exercises to complete the side-by-side notes below. Include only the two points from the reading and the listening that clearly contract each other.

| READING | LISTENING |
|---|---|
| **Main Idea** | **Main Idea** |
| *Paying employees on commission benefits* | *Not all employees should be* |
| | |
| **First Supporting Argument** | **First Supporting Argument** |
| *Offering employees commission-based* | *Some jobs cannot or should not be* |
| *payments* | |
| Supporting Detail | Supporting Detail |
| | |
| **Second Supporting Argument** | **Second Supporting Argument** |
| *Employees who work on commission can* | *Being paid on commission does not always* |
| | |
| Supporting Detail | Supporting Detail |
| | |

Use this page to write your response. You have 20 minutes to complete your essay.

## Writing Guide

Summarize the points made in the lecture, being sure to explain how they challenge specific claims made in the reading passage.

**First Paragraph** ▷

State and discuss thesis

**Second Paragraph** ▷

First main idea from lecture

Supporting detail

Contradiction from reading

**Third Paragraph** ▷

Second main idea from lecture

Supporting detail

Contradiction from reading

**Fourth Paragraph** ▷

Conclusion (optional)

---

**Scaffolding**   Here are some useful phrases to help you when you write.

> The reading passage and the lecture deal with…

> The professor, however, asserts…

> First, the lecturer explains that…

> His argument call into question the one made in the…

> Next, the instructor states that…

> To explain this, he talks about…

> On the other hand, the reading passage claims that…

The reading passage and the lecture deal with the issue of paying staff on commission. The reading passage states that commission-based payments benefit both employers and employees. The professor, however, asserts that paying on commission might not benefit all workers.

The lecturer begins by stating that not all jobs should be paid according to the amount of work completed. He gives the example of teachers. He argues that teachers should not be paid on commission because the quality of education would decrease substantially. His argument calls into question the one made in the reading passage. There, it is stated that paying employees based on the amount of work they do leads them to work more efficiently and to do better jobs than employees earning flat salaries.

The professor also believes that employees paid on commission do not always make more money. He says that the amount of money an employee on commission earns can fluctuate greatly each month. In some months, they can make a lot of money. In other months, they might make none at all. This often makes people uncomfortable about their financial situations. On the other hand, the reading passage claims that employees earn much more money and are happier receiving commission-based salaries.

| **Critical Analysis** | Refer to the sample response to complete the tasks below.

1   Underline the topic sentence in each paragraph.

2   Double underline the sentences that refer to the listening.

3   Which word in the response means "**unchanging**"? Write the word on the line below.

_____

4   What does "**fluctuate greatly**" mean? Find the sentence that explains this and write it on the lines below.

_____

_____

5   List at least two of the transitions the writer uses on the lines below.

_____

_____

_____

The lecture that came after the reading passage gave some argument in against commission salaries. The lectuers arguments casted some doubt on the reading passage.

Firstly, the lecture said that some people should not be pay on commission. The he stated was about teacher. He said teachers get paid on commission only them benefit. Clearly, this is not a good solution. For these types of job, commission payment is not a good idea. This is contrasting the reading passage, where it argued that workers on commission completere their tasks more quickly.

Next, the professor dis proves the argument about salary increase on commissions. He says that only sometimes does salary increase. Othertimes, the salary can be virtually none. He argues that this changing salary makes workers less productivity. However, the reading passage argued otherwise. It states that employees who are getting commission earn double to triple their salary. From this, it is clear this not always true.

| **Critical Analysis** |   Refer to the sample response to complete the tasks below.

**1**   In which of the following ways should the highlighted sentence be rewritten?

(A)  The professor contends that constantly fluctuating salaries make workers less productive.

(B)  In the lecture, the instructor talks about the importance of salaries and work productivity.

(C)  The lecturer argues that employees with low productivity often earn changing salaries.

**2**   Where should the following sentence be added to improve the response?

**For instance, teachers who are paid based on the number of students that pass their classes would never fail any students.**

(A)  Introductory paragraph

(B)  Body paragraph 1

(C)  Body paragraph 2

**3**   Find at least two grammatical mistakes in the response. Write the corrected sentences on the lines below.

_____

_____

_____

# Working at a High-Paying Job with Low Security

 Would you prefer to work at a high-paying job that does not offer job security, or would you prefer to work at a lower-paying but secure job? Use specific reasons and details to support your choice.

## Generating Ideas

The following questions will help you write your response. Answer each with one or two sentences. Plan an answer for both options. Some ideas have been provided to help you.

### Idea Box    High-Paying Job

**1 Q** What are the practical benefits of earning more money?

**A** *By earning more money, a person does not have to worry about paying bills or buying food.*

**2 Q** How can changing jobs often be beneficial?

**A** *Changing jobs can often make a person's life*

**3 Q** How does earning a high salary improve a person's quality of life?

**A** *With a high salary,*

Reason 1:

Reason 2:

### Idea Box    Secure Job

**1 Q** In what ways can job security be better than earning a lot of money?

**A** *Having a secure job makes it possible to plan for the future, which money alone cannot do.*

**2 Q** What are the drawbacks of not having a secure long-term job?

**A** *A person could never become*

**3 Q** Does a person need a high salary to be happy? Explain.

**A** *No, having a lot of money does not matter*

Reason 1:

Reason 2:

## Developing Ideas

Having examined the two options, which do you feel more comfortable developing into an essay? Explain why you feel this way.

Use the outline to plan your response to the following: Would you prefer to work at a high-paying job that does not offer job security, or would you prefer to work at a lower-paying but secure job? Use specific reasons and details to support your choice.

### High-Paying Job

**Thesis Statement**

*I would prefer to work at a high-paying job with little job security.*

**First Supporting Idea**

**Supporting Example**

**Second Supporting Idea**

**Supporting Example**

**Conclusion**

### Secure Job

**Thesis Statement**

*I would rather have a secure job even if it did not pay a lot of money.*

**First Supporting Idea**

**Supporting Example**

**Second Supporting Idea**

**Supporting Example**

**Conclusion**

Use this page to write your response. You have 30 minutes to complete your essay.

**Writing Guide**

Would you prefer to work at a high-paying job that does not offer job security, or would you prefer to work at a lower-paying but secure job? Use specific reasons and details to support your choice.

**First Paragraph** ○

State and discuss thesis

**Second Paragraph** ○

First main supporting idea

Supporting detail

Example

**Third Paragraph** ○

Second main supporting idea

Supporting detail

Example

**Fourth Paragraph** ○

Conclusion

**Scaffolding** Here are some useful phrases to help you when you write.

> It is for this reason that I would prefer…

> For one, the amount of money a person earns…

> Earning a high salary is not as important as…

> This has certainly been the case with…

> Furthermore, making a lot of money does (not)…

> To illustrate, let me recount…

> Although some people may prefer… for people like me… are the way to go.

Our jobs serve many important functions in our lives. They give us a sense of purpose. They provide us with ways to learn new things and to develop new skills. But perhaps most importantly, they allow us to earn money and to make a living. It is for this reason that I would prefer to work at a higher-paying job that offers less job security.

For one, the amount of money a person earns directly affects that person's quality of life. Simply put, the more money someone earns, the better that person's life will be. This has certainly been the case with my older brother. He works as a manager at a major company and earns a very large paycheck. As a result, he is able to afford many nice things for himself. For instance, he lives in a large apartment in a wealthy part of the city, drives a luxury car, and wears only the best clothing. Although some people may think these sorts of things are unnecessary, they allow him to live a better life. This, in turn, positively affects his health and happiness. This is why earning a higher salary is better than earning a lower salary.

In addition, finding another job is not difficult. At any given time, there are large numbers of jobs available, especially for people with specialized training living in large cities. To illustrate, let me recount one of my friend's experiences. Not long ago, she graduated from college with a degree in engineering. She was quickly able to get a job with a starting salary of 50,000 dollars per year. She worked at that job for six months until she was suddenly fired one day. Within a month, my friend was able to find a similar position with even better pay. Since then, she has worked at four different jobs, each one with better pay and benefits. For people with skills that are in demand, job security is not a concern.

Some people place great value on living stable lives. For these people, low-paying but secure jobs are superior. However, for people like me who enjoy earning a lot of money and do not mind changing jobs every few years, higher-paying jobs with less job security are the way to go.

| **Critical Analysis** | Refer to the sample response to complete the tasks below.

1   Underline the topic sentence in each paragraph.

2   Double underline the sentences that include supporting details.

3   List at least two of the examples the writer uses on the lines below.

_____

_____

_____

People worry about money. They think money will solve problem. But sometimes, money is problem by it self. Some people might like a big money job. But I think low pay job is can be better.

Sometimes low pay jobs are ok. They can have comfortable, and this makes life comfortable. Like you stay at the same job for a lot of time. Then you have comfortable life. If you change the job every so often then you do not have the comfortable. **1** It is good just to stay in one place, sometimes. Even though high pay job seems good idea its really not so much.

And also, money is not always so important. You have enough money, then its ok. You don't have extravagent life style, but you are not needed that. **2** You can be happy the way you are. For example, if you make the 2,000 dollar a month you pay the rent. You eat the food when become hungry. And this is not problem, because you have comfortable. **3**

Having the comfort is most crucial. So therefore the low pay job can be better.

---

| **Critical Analysis** |   Refer to the sample response to complete the tasks below.

1   Where should the following sentence be added to improve the response?

**A person does not need to drive a luxury car in order to be happy.**

  Ⓐ **1**

  Ⓑ **2**

  Ⓒ **3**

2   The topic sentence from the second body paragraph is not clear. Rewrite it to make it clearer.

3   Think of at least one supporting idea to add to the second body paragraph to make it more interesting.

4   Find at least two grammatical mistakes in the response. Write the corrected sentences on the lines below.

# Part B

# Communication: **Interactive Voice Response Technology**

**🔊 Vocabulary** Take a few moments to review the vocabulary items that will appear in this task.

**interactive** *adj.* acting or capable of acting on each other or together

Video games are enjoyable because they are **interactive**.

**recognize** *v.* to remember the identity of a person or thing

I am sorry, but I do not **recognize** you. Are you sure that we have met before?

**in conjunction with** *prep.* together with

My school is hosting the soccer competition **in conjunction with** other schools in the area.

**screen** *v.* to separate a group into smaller parts

Employers **screen** possible workers based on their work history.

**segment** *v.* to make several different parts in order

In order to understand the information, you must **segment** it into related parts.

**representative** *n.* an individual who speaks or acts in place of others

I will not be able to attend the meeting, so I will have to send a **representative**.

**anonymous** *adj.* without a known name

Celebrities who want to remain **anonymous** in public wear sunglasses to hide their faces.

**survey** *n.* a gathering of a sample of data or opinions considered to be representative of a whole

The restaurant will conduct a customer satisfaction **survey** to improve service.

**moderate** *adj.* being within reasonable limits; not extreme

Drinking a **moderate** amount of alcohol can actually be healthy for you.

## Reading

Read the passage carefully. Try to understand what the main argument of the passage is. You have 3 minutes to read.

Interactive voice response technology, otherwise known as IVR technology, is one of the most widely used telephone technologies today. It works by using a system that recognizes different dial sounds in conjunction with voice menus. Without IVR technology, modern telecommunications would not be possible.

First, IVR technology allows companies to make their services more efficient. Company call centers rely on the technology to screen and segment callers. When customers contact a call center, the IVR system requires them to answer a few questions about the type of service they want. The system then connects callers to the appropriate information center. This allows call centers to be able to provide faster and more efficient service. Rather than waiting to speak to a representative, callers can receive immediate service thanks to IVR technology.

In addition, IVR systems allow callers to remain anonymous. Due to this, IVR systems allow information to be exchanged more accurately. This is especially true in situations during which callers might not be comfortable with speaking to a human representative. One example of this would be a survey about voting. When asked by a person to give their opinions about political topics, people are more likely to give moderate answers. When asked the same questions by an IVR system, people generally give their honest opinions. When privacy and accuracy are the main concerns, IVR systems are superior.

| **Paraphrasing** | The following sentences come from the reading passage. Complete each paraphrase with appropriate words or phrases.

1   When customers contact a call center, the IVR system requires them to answer a few questions about the type of service they want.

→ *IVR systems will present callers* _____ *to determine*

_____ *they require.*

2   Rather than waiting to speak to a representative, callers are able to receive immediate service thanks to IVR technology.

→ *With IVR systems, callers do not have to* _____ *when they phone a call center.*

3   This is especially true in situations during which callers might not be comfortable with speaking to a human representative.

→ *These systems are* _____ *when callers would rather not*

_____ .

4   When asked by a person to give their opinions about political topics, people are more likely to give moderate answers.

→ *Callers tend not to give their* _____ *when talking to*

_____ .

| **Summarizing** | Complete the summary below by using the information from the reading passage. Be sure to paraphrase the information.

In the reading passage, the writer asserts that _____ in modern telecommunications. The author's first argument is that IVR systems make call center services more efficient. This is illustrated by the fact that these systems _____ and connect them to _____ more quickly. The writer's next argument is that IVR technology allows information to be exchanged _____ . The reason is that callers are more honest when dealing with one of these systems.

## 🔵 Vocabulary  Take a few moments to review the vocabulary items that will appear in this task.

**despise**  *v.* to dislike strongly; to scorn

I like most foods, but I **despise** tomatoes.

**hinder**  *v.* to be or get in the way of; to obstruct

Our trip was **hindered** by the snowstorm.

**series**  *n.* a number of things placed or occurring one after the other

There is a **series** of tasks you must complete to get the job.

**previous**  *adj.* happening before in time or order

You should complete the **previous** chapter before moving on to the next one.

**navigate**  *v.* to move through the menu arrangement in a software program

Newer computer programs are much easier to **navigate** than older ones.

**impersonal**  *adj.* feeling or showing no strong emotional involvement

When grading a student's work, teachers should remain **impersonal**.

**application**  *n.* a way of being used

Personal computers have many different **applications**. They can be used to write papers, to surf the Internet, to watch movies, and to do much more.

**deal with**  *phr v.* to do business with someone

International businesspeople have to **deal with** clients from all over the world.

**insignificant**  *adj.* not important; of no consequence

Thanks to the Internet, people feel the need to share every **insignificant** detail of their lives with the world.

## Listening

Now listen to part of a lecture on the topic you just read about.

02-08

**1**  But rather than improving customer service, these systems actually hinder it.

→ *Not only do IVR systems fail to _____, but they actually _____.*

**2**  Sometimes these menus are not organized well, so it can be difficult to determine which button you need to press.

→ *The menus in IVR are not always _____, which makes it _____ the information you need.*

**3**  Simply put, it is much easier to get an answer from a person than to try to navigate a series of confusing prerecorded menus.

→ *It is simpler to get information _____ than to search through _____.*

**4**  They know that customer satisfaction is more important than saving a bit of money with these IVR systems.

→ *Companies understand that _____ is not as important as _____.*

| **Summarizing** | Complete the summary below by using the information from the lecture. Be sure to paraphrase the information.

In his lecture, the instructor _____ because they worsen customer service. He supports his opinion with two main ideas. The first is that IVR technology _____. This is due to the fact that callers have to navigate _____ that are sometimes not organized very well. He also dislikes IVR systems for being _____. He says that most people would rather speak to another person, and it is for this reason that many companies are now _____ call centers.

Refer to the paraphrasing and summarizing exercises to complete the side-by-side notes below. Include only the two points from the reading and the listening that clearly contract each other.

| READING | LISTENING |
|---|---|
| **Main Idea** | **Main Idea** |
| *Modern telecommunications would not be* | *IVR systems do not* |
| **First Supporting Argument** | **First Supporting Argument** |
| *IVR systems allow companies to* | *This technology does not* |
| Supporting Detail | Supporting Detail |
| **Second Supporting Argument** | **Second Supporting Argument** |
| *These systems allow callers to* | *IVR systems are too* |
| Supporting Detail | Supporting Detail |

Use this page to write your response. You have 20 minutes to complete your essay.

| Writing Guide | Summarize the points made in the lecture, being sure to explain how they cast doubt on specific points made in the reading passage. |
|---|---|
| **First Paragraph** ○<br><br>State and discuss thesis | |
| **Second Paragraph** ○<br><br>First main idea from lecture<br><br>Contradiction from reading<br><br>Supporting detail | |
| **Third Paragraph** ○<br><br>Second main idea from lecture<br><br>Contradiction from reading<br><br>Supporting detail | |
| **Fourth Paragraph** ○<br><br>Conclusion (optional) | |

**⑤ Scaffolding**   Here are some useful phrases to help you when you write.

> The topic of the reading passage and the lecture is…

> The reading passage presents arguments strongly in favor of… but the lecturer questions…

> First, the reading passage claims…

> The professor starts his lecture by…

> The lecturer calls this argument into…

> The instructor goes on to talk about…

> This statement that… rebuts the assertion made in the reading passage that…

The topic of the reading passage and the lecture is interactive voice response technology. The reading passage presents arguments strongly in favor of this technology, but the lecturer disputes the validity of these arguments.

First, the reading passage claims that IVR systems help callers save time because they help call centers provide personalized service for each caller. The lecturer calls this argument into question. He states that IVR systems do not make telecommunication services more efficient because they require callers to waste time navigating menus to find the information they seek. He goes on to say that most callers would feel more comfortable talking to an actual person.

Then, to refute the reading passage's assertion that the anonymity of IVR systems is a benefit, the instructor criticizes IVR systems for being too impersonal. He says these systems can make callers feel unimportant and insignificant. The professor explains that many call centers are now switching back to human representatives because they know providing good customer service is better than saving money.

| Critical Analysis | Refer to the sample response to complete the tasks below.

1 Underline the topic sentence in each paragraph.

2 Double underline the sentences that refer to the listening.

3 Which word in the response means "**without a known name**"? Write the word on the line below.

_____

4 What does "**insignificant**" mean? Find the sentence that explains this and write it on the lines below.

_____

_____

5 List at least two of the transitions the writer uses on the lines below.

_____

_____

_____

At the article, it argued that IVR systems are need today in telecommunications. It gave some arguments in favor of this.

First, the IVR system lets companies service more quickly. The system let customers answer there questions quickly. This is faster than speaking to representative, according to the passage. **1** The speaking said this was not true however. **2** He said the systems are too confusion to use. **3** And they have to press to many button. So in this way they are worse.

Second, the IVR system allow callers to exchange more accuratey. This is true when the human representative is not comfortable. One example of this is about voting. There IVR system are better. Lecture said against this though. He said IVR system are not want. Most people want to speak to human being on the phone. In this way the systems are not a smart choice to make.

| **Critical Analysis** | Refer to the sample response to complete the tasks below.

1. In which of the following ways should the highlighted sentence be rewritten?

   (A) According to the professor, fewer people are confused thanks to the use of IVR systems.

   (B) In the lecture, it is stated that IVR technology is not as complex as it used to be.

   (C) The lecturer argues that IVR systems are too confusing to use easily.

2. Where should the following sentence be added to improve the response?

   **The menus make it difficult for a person to find the information he or she is searching for.**

   (A) **1**

   (B) **2**

   (C) **3**

3. Find at least two grammatical mistakes in the response. Write the corrected sentences on the lines below.

_____

_____

_____

# A Person Working in a Group Must Accept Criticism

 Do you agree or disagree with the following statement? A person cannot work successfully in a group if that individual cannot accept criticism. Use specific reasons and examples to support your answer.

## Generating Ideas

The following questions will help you write your response. Answer each with one or two sentences. Plan an answer for both options. Some ideas have been provided to help you.

### Idea Box   Agree

**1 Q** What is the purpose of working in a group?

**A** *The purpose is to generate many ideas from different people and to use the best ideas.*

**2 Q** If a group has a stubborn member, how can it be more difficult to finish a task?

**A** *It would become*

**3 Q** How can one person who does not accept criticism affect the success of the entire group?

**A** *This person can*

Reason 1:

Reason 2:

### Idea Box   Disagree

**1 Q** How can disagreements help a group achieve its goals more easily?

**A** *A group can save time because its members will not spend time arguing over ideas.*

**2 Q** What are some justifiable reasons a person might not listen to criticism from others?

**A** *The person may know*

**3 Q** In what ways can a stubborn group member enable a group to be more successful?

**A** *It can*

Reason 1:

Reason 2:

## Developing Ideas

Having examined the two options, which do you feel more comfortable developing into an essay? Explain why you feel this way.

Use the outline to plan your response to the following: Do you agree or disagree with the following statement? A person cannot work successfully in a group if that individual cannot accept criticism. Use specific reasons and examples to support your answer.

## Agree

**Thesis Statement**

*I entirely agree that a person cannot work successfully in a group if that individual cannot accept criticism.*

**First Supporting Idea**

Supporting Example

**Second Supporting Idea**

Supporting Example

**Conclusion**

## Disagree

**Thesis Statement**

*I contend that a person can contribute to a group successfully even if that individual cannot accept criticism.*

**First Supporting Idea**

Supporting Example

**Second Supporting Idea**

Supporting Example

**Conclusion**

Use this page to write your response. You have 30 minutes to complete your essay.

| Writing Guide | Do you agree or disagree with the following statement? A person cannot work successfully in a group if that individual cannot accept criticism. Use specific reasons and examples to support your answer. |
|---|---|

**First Paragraph** ○

State and discuss thesis

**Second Paragraph** ○

First main supporting idea

Supporting detail

Example

**Third Paragraph** ○

Second main supporting idea

Supporting detail

Example

**Fourth Paragraph** ○

Conclusion

**◔ Scaffolding**   Here are some useful phrases to help you when you write.

> I entirely agree/completely disagree with the statement that…

> From these experiences, I have learned that…

> When working in a group, it is important that…

> I will illustrate with a personal…

> Furthermore, a person who cannot… will lower the quality…

> In addition, people who do not listen to criticism…

> From this experience, I can say for sure that…

> Overall, I believe that…

I entirely agree with the statement that a person cannot work successfully in a group if that individual cannot accept criticism. Throughout my years as a student, I have worked on many group projects. From these experiences, I have learned that in order to be successful, the members of a group have to be flexible and open to new ideas.

When working in a group, it is important that all members work together to complete their task. If a person is unwilling to accept criticism, then the group may not finish on time. This happened to a group I was working in during high school. There was one member of my group who would not listen to our suggestions about how to improve her ideas. She would often become angry if we did not completely agree with her. Eventually, she refused to do any more work for the group. As a result, the rest of us had to do our work and hers, so we were not able to finish our assignment on time.

Furthermore, a person who cannot accept criticism will lower the quality of the work produced by the entire group. If one person in a group does a bad job, then all of the members are affected. This happened when I had to give a group presentation in my literature class. One member of my group refused to let any of us edit his speech, which contained several mistakes. When our group finally gave our presentation, most of us did well, except for the stubborn member. In the end, our group got a B for our presentation. Had the one member listened to our suggestions, we might have gotten an A. From this experience, I can say for sure that groups suffer when one member does not accept criticism.

Overall, I believe that in order to be successful in a group, a person must be willing to accept criticism. A person who is unwilling to accept criticism will make whole group suffer. That is why a successful group is one in which all the members are able to work together effectively.

| Critical Analysis | Refer to the sample response to complete the tasks below.

1   Underline the topic sentence in each paragraph.

2   Double underline the sentences that include supporting details.

3   List at least two of the examples the writer uses on the lines below.

_____

_____

_____

When you do work, sometimes you have to do group work. You have to work as a partner in a group. This has good points and bad points. Some people think that work in a group means taking the criticism but it not always so.

First, giving the criticism take the time and groups do not have a lot of time to spend so it is better to avoid the criticism in total. Like consider the group who thinks about its ideas so much then how they do their work. In actual they don't do their work much because they waste time talking about ideas without doing the work. So in this way criticism is the wasting time. In this case just work without criticism does the complete more effectively. My brother was a group for work once. He did his ideas and make the work. He could not hear the others talking for his work. He just worked as he wanted and his ideas were not too bad. In the last they did it on time and even though it was not criticism he group had a big success.

Last the member of the goup does not hear the criticism for a good reason, because his ideas are too good for to listen. The leader does not accept the criticism form others if it is no good because it does not fooled. Like my group where one did not hear the criticism. He just do his work whatever he wanted. We said him your ideas are no good and they will fail but it turns out they were ok. After we did complete project he stopped to tell us that we got perfect score. So in this way arguing his points would have waisted the time therefore it was benefit that he could not hear criticism.

When the group work happens it can be bad. It can have problems arise and this is why criticism should be avoided. In other words working a group without criticism can have beneficial.

---

| **Critical Analysis** |   Refer to the sample response to complete the tasks below.

1   Which of the following sentences could be added to strengthen the response?

   (A) My brother did not listen to the criticisms of his group members because he was confident in his ideas.

   (B) People who refuse to listen to criticism often do work of lower quality than those who do listen.

   (C) The stubborn member eventually left the group, and this made it easier for us to finish more quickly.

2   The topic sentence in the second body paragraph is not clear. Rewrite it to make it clearer.

3   Think of at least one supporting idea to add to the first body paragraph to make it more interesting.

4   Find at least two grammatical mistakes in the response. Write the corrected sentences on the lines below.

_____

_____

_____

# Part C

# Experiencing the TOEFL iBT Actual Tests

# Writing Section Directions

 **Make sure your headset is on.**

This section measures your ability to use writing to communicate in an academic environment. There will be two writing tasks.

For the first writing task, you will read a passage and listen to a lecture and then answer a question based on what you have read and heard. For the second writing task, you will answer a question based on your own knowledge and experience.

Now listen to the directions for the first writing task.

03-01

## Task 1

# Writing Based on Reading and Listening

03-02

For this task, you will first have **3 minutes** to read a passage about an academic topic. You may take notes on the passage if you wish. The passage will then be removed and you will listen to a lecture about the same topic. While you listen, you may also take notes.

Then you will have **20 minutes** to write a response to a question that asks you about the relationship between the lecture you heard and the reading passage. Try to answer the question as completely as possible using information from the reading passage and the lecture. The question does **not** ask you to express your personal opinion. You will be able to see the reading passage again when it is time for you to write. You may use your notes to help you answer the question.

Typically, an effective response will be 150 to 250 words long. Your response will be judged on the quality of your writing and on the completeness and accuracy of the content. If you finish your response before time is up, you may click on **Next** to go on to the second writing task.

Now you will see the reading passage for 3 minutes. Remember it will be available to you again while you are writing. Immediately after the reading time ends, the lecture will begin, so keep your headset on until the lecture is over.

Throughout history, humans have searched for ways to preserve food. From salt curing to canning, each method preserves food in different ways. In 1958, a German scientist introduced the world to a new method called food irradiation, which exposes food to nuclear radiation. When considering its benefits, it is clear that governments around the world need to make food irradiation mandatory.

During the irradiation process, insects and microscopic organisms on the food are killed. This is easily the primary advantage of food irradiation. The benefits of killing these organisms are twofold. First, killing the organisms that live on food makes it safer to eat. As a result, the risk of getting ill from food is drastically reduced. Second, because the insects are dead, they cannot destroy supplies of food that are waiting to be sold.

Food irradiation benefits consumer health in other ways, too. Food that is not preserved can lose vitamins and nutrients over time. Other preservation methods such as freezing or canning have been shown to destroy some nutrients. Irradiation, however, perfectly preserves the nutrients in food by stopping the aging process at the optimal time.

Not only does irradiation make food healthier, but it also makes food last longer. When the radiation changes the food's atoms, it slows down the growth of the food. For example, a regular banana from the grocery store may last one week before it goes bad. An irradiated banana, on the other hand, can stay fresh for months. This is good news for both growers and consumers of food. Consumers will not need to throw out rotten fruits and vegetables if they are irradiated. Additionally, farmers and grocery stores will not lose their investments if no one buys their products within a few days.

03-03

**Directions** You have 20 minutes to plan and write your response. Your response will be judged on the basis of the quality of your writing and on how well your response presents the points in the lecture and their relationship to the reading passage. Typically, an effective response will be 150 to 225 words.

**Question** Summarize the main points in the lecture, being sure to explain how they cast doubt on specific points made in the reading passage.

Throughout history, humans have searched for ways to preserve food. From salt curing to canning, each method preserves food in different ways. In 1958, a German scientist introduced the world to a new method called food irradiation, which exposes food to nuclear radiation. When considering its benefits, it is clear that governments around the world need to make food irradiation mandatory.

During the irradiation process, insects and microscopic organisms on the food are killed. This is easily the primary advantage of food irradiation. The benefits of killing these organisms are twofold. First, killing the organisms that live on food makes it safer to eat. As a result, the risk of getting ill from food is drastically reduced. Second, because the insects are dead, they cannot destroy supplies of food that are waiting to be sold.

Food irradiation benefits consumer health in other ways, too. Food that is not preserved can lose vitamins and nutrients over time. Other preservation methods such as freezing or canning have been shown to destroy some nutrients. Irradiation, however, perfectly preserves the nutrients in food by stopping the aging process at the optimal time.

Not only does irradiation make food healthier, but it also makes food last longer. When the radiation changes the food's atoms, it slows down the growth of the food. For example, a regular banana from the grocery store may last one week before it goes bad. An irradiated banana, on the other hand, can stay fresh for months. This is good news for both growers and consumers of food. Consumers will not need to throw out rotten fruits and vegetables if they are irradiated. Additionally, farmers and grocery stores will not lose their investments if no one buys their products within a few days.

## Task 2

# Writing Based on
# Knowledge and Experience

For this task, you will write an essay in response to a question that asks you to state, explain, and support your opinion on an issue. You will have **30 minutes** to write your essay.

Typically, an effective essay will contain a minimum of 300 words. Your essay will be judged on the quality of your writing. This includes the development of your ideas, the organization of your essay, and the quality and accuracy of the language you use to express ideas.

Click on **Continue** to go on.

**Directions** Read the question below. You have 30 minutes to plan, write, and revise your essay. Typically, an effective response will contain a minimum of 300 words.

### Question

Do you agree or disagree with the following statement?

**The government should increase the price of electricity in order to encourage people to conserve it.**

Use specific reasons and examples to support your answer.

CONTINUE    VOLUME

# Writing Section Directions

 **Make sure your headset is on.**

This section measures your ability to use writing to communicate in an academic environment. There will be two writing tasks.

For the first writing task, you will read a passage and listen to a lecture and then answer a question based on what you have read and heard. For the second writing task, you will answer a question based on your own knowledge and experience.

Now listen to the directions for the first writing task.

## Task 1

# Writing Based on Reading and Listening

03-06

For this task, you will first have **3 minutes** to read a passage about an academic topic. You may take notes on the passage if you wish. The passage will then be removed and you will listen to a lecture about the same topic. While you listen, you may also take notes.

Then you will have **20 minutes** to write a response to a question that asks you about the relationship between the lecture you heard and the reading passage. Try to answer the question as completely as possible using information from the reading passage and the lecture. The question does **not** ask you to express your personal opinion. You will be able to see the reading passage again when it is time for you to write. You may use your notes to help you answer the question.

Typically, an effective response will be 150 to 250 words long. Your response will be judged on the quality of your writing and on the completeness and accuracy of the content. If you finish your response before time is up, you may click on **Next** to go on to the second writing task.

Now you will see the reading passage for 3 minutes. Remember it will be available to you again while you are writing. Immediately after the reading time ends, the lecture will begin, so keep your headset on until the lecture is over.

In numerous countries in Europe and North America, various traffic problems could be solved easily. These countries simply need to build high-speed trains to connect their major cities and suburbs. These trains would provide numerous benefits wherever they are constructed.

Some high-speed trains can exceed speeds of 400 kilometers per hour. Many others are capable of moving 200 kilometers per hour or more. If more of these types of trains are constructed, then people will realize they can arrive at their destinations, such as their workplaces, very quickly. Large numbers of commuters will stop driving to their workplaces. This will reduce traffic jams, which will let people who still drive reach their destinations faster than usual.

If more people take trains and fewer people drive, there will be less wear and tear on roads. This will reduce the need for road maintenance. Nowadays, large cities and suburbs spend large sums of money from their budgets on road maintenance. This is particularly true of places that get heavy rains or lots of snowy weather. There are seemingly roadwork crews working constantly throughout these cities to repair streets. This will be unnecessary when high-speed trains become a preferred method of transportation.

High-speed trains are also relatively inexpensive. The reason is that they are very fuel efficient. When these trains are operating, they use a fairly small amount of energy despite their high speeds. This makes them cheap to operate once they are constructed.

It is imperative for governments in Europe and North America to construct more high-speed railways. They will provide a large number of benefits to society. They will reduce traffic, lessen the need for road maintenance, and save money due to their fuel-efficient nature. These are tremendous advantages that countries should take advantage of.

03-07

**Directions** You have 20 minutes to plan and write your response. Your response will be judged on the basis of the quality of your writing and on how well your response presents the points in the lecture and their relationship to the reading passage. Typically, an effective response will be 150 to 225 words.

**Question** Summarize the points made in the lecture, being sure to explain how they challenge specific claims made in the reading passage.

---

In numerous countries in Europe and North America, various traffic problems could be solved easily. These countries simply need to build high-speed trains to connect their major cities and suburbs. These trains would provide numerous benefits wherever they are constructed.

Some high-speed trains can exceed speeds of 400 kilometers per hour. Many others are capable of moving 200 kilometers per hour or more. If more of these types of trains are constructed, then people will realize they can arrive at their destinations, such as their workplaces, very quickly. Large numbers of commuters will stop driving to their workplaces. This will reduce traffic jams, which will let people who still drive reach their destinations faster than usual.

If more people take trains and fewer people drive, there will be less wear and tear on roads. This will reduce the need for road maintenance. Nowadays, large cities and suburbs spend large sums of money from their budgets on road maintenance. This is particularly true of places that get heavy rains or lots of snowy weather. There are seemingly roadwork crews working constantly throughout these cities to repair streets. This will be unnecessary when high-speed trains become a preferred method of transportation.

High-speed trains are also relatively inexpensive. The reason is that they are very fuel efficient. When these trains are operating, they use a fairly small amount of energy despite their high speeds. This makes them cheap to operate once they are constructed.

It is imperative for governments in Europe and North America to construct more high-speed railways. They will provide a large number of benefits to society. They will reduce traffic, lessen the need for road maintenance, and save money due to their fuel-efficient nature. These are tremendous advantages that countries should take advantage of.

## Task 2

# Writing Based on
# Knowledge and Experience

03-08

For this task, you will write an essay in response to a question that asks you to state, explain, and support your opinion on an issue. You will have **30 minutes** to write your essay.

Typically, an effective essay will contain a minimum of 300 words. Your essay will be judged on the quality of your writing. This includes the development of your ideas, the organization of your essay, and the quality and accuracy of the language you use to express ideas.

Click on **Continue** to go on.

**Directions** Read the question below. You have 30 minutes to plan, write, and revise your essay. Typically, an effective response will contain a minimum of 300 words.

## Question

Do you agree or disagree with the following statement?

**It is more important for a teacher to try to help students gain self-confidence than to teach them specific knowledge.**

Use specific reasons and examples to support your answer.

# Appendix

# MASTER
# WORD LIST

# MASTER WORD LIST

## Chapter 01

**aggressively** *adv.* forcefully; hostilely; in a hostile manner

**ancestor** *n.* a forefather; a person coming early in the family line

**captivity** *n.* the act of keeping animals

**conclude** *v.* to reach a decision about; to decide

**creature** *n.* a living organism, especially an animal

**genetic** *adj.* relating to the science of heredity, which is the study of how parents pass their characteristics on to their children

**harmony** *n.* social agreement

**intense** *adj.* extreme in degree, strength, or size

**invalid** *adj.* not based on the truth; worthless

**primate** *n.* an animal such as a monkey, an ape, or a human being

**react** *v.* to act in response to something; to respond

**resolve** *v.* to find a solution to a problem or argument

**resort to** *phr v.* to look to when in need

**shocking** *adj.* very surprising; outrageous

**tranquil** *adj.* calm; peaceful

**zoologist** *n.* a scientist who studies animals and animal life

## Chapter 02

**adjacent** *adj.* close to; next to

**ambitious** *adj.* having a strong desire to be successful

**challenge** *v.* to question; to face up to

**command** *v.* to give orders to; to control

**demise** *n.* the end of the existence of someone or something; death

**destabilize** *v.* to weaken the power of a government

**drought** *n.* a long period of no rain

**famine** *n.* an extreme shortage of food

**greedy** *adj.* wanting or taking all that one can get with no thought of what others need

**influence** *n.* the power to act on or to affect people or things

**irrigate** *v.* to water crops

**loyal** *adj.* faithful to one's family, duty, country, or beliefs

**revolt** *n.* to attempt to overthrow the authority of the state; to rebel

**suffer** *v.* to experience something painful

**tremendous** *adj.* extremely large in amount, extent, or degree; enormous

**unquestioned** *adj.* accepted without question

**uprising** *n.* a rebellion against a government; a revolt

**widespread** *adj.* spread out over a large area; pervasive

## Chapter 03

**convincing** *adj.* causing one to believe that something is true; persuasive

**conduct** *v.* to organize and do a task

**decrease** *v.* to become smaller in size, number, or amount

**determine** *v.* to decide something

**dramatically** *adv.* to a great degree or large amount

**draw in** *phr v.* to breathe in deeply; to take in

**efficiently** *adv.* proficiently; effectively

**focused** *adj.* concentrating on something

**frequency** *n.* the number of times something happens during a specific amount of time

**generate** *v.* to produce; to make

**inactivity** *n.* the state of being idle; not doing an activity

**increase** *v.* to become larger in size, number, or amount

**mystery** *n.* something that is not known or explained or that is kept secret

**propose** *v.* to make a suggestion

**proven** *adj.* known to be true

**regulate** *v.* to control an activity, usually with a set of rules

**result** *n.* something that comes about as an effect or end

**theory** *n.* a set of ideas created to explain why something happens

## Chapter 04

**consequence** *n.* something that happens as a result of an event

**contribute** *v.* to work together with others to achieve a common goal

**deserve** *v.* to be worthy of; to earn

**developed nation** *n.* a nation with a high level of economic development

**elsewhere** *adv.* in other places; in another place

**estimate** *v.* to make a general but careful guess about the size, value, or cost of something

**follow suit** *phr v.* to do as someone else has done; to imitate

**funding** *n.* money given to pay for something specific

**indirect** *adj.* not straight; by a longer way

**insist** *v.* to demand or say in a strong, firm manner

**run into** *phr v.* to cost a lot of money

**skyrocket** *v.* suddenly to increase by a very large amount

**suitably** *adj.* appropriately; correctly

**topnotch** *adj.* of the highest quality; excellent

**tuition** *n.* money paid for education, especially at a college or university

**unattainable** *adj.* not able to be reached; not available

**unintended** *adj.* not meant to be done; unplanned

## Chapter 05

**accommodate** *v.* to hold comfortably without crowding

**ancient** *adj.* very old; lasting a long time

**archaeologist** *n.* a scientist who studies past cultures and people

**artifact** *n.* an object made by human beings, especially a tool or weapon of archaeological interest

**constellation** *n.* a group of stars that appears to form an image in the sky

**fascinating** *adj.* pleasing to the eye or mind

**highway** *n.* a main road that usually connects different cities

**honor** *v.* to show respect toward

**means** *n.* how a result is obtained or an end is achieved

**mound** *n.* a pile of earth, gravel, sand, or rocks

**put forth** *phr v.* to suggest something

**seldom** *adv.* not often; infrequently; rarely

**significance** *n.* having importance or a special meaning

**solely** *adv.* only; entirely

**stretch** *v.* to reach; to extend

**transportation** *n.* the act of moving people or things around

**unnecessarily** *adv.* possible to do without; not needed

**vehicle** *n.* a machine that is used for transporting people or goods

## Chapter 06

**attractive** *adj.* good looking; beautiful

**bark** *n.* the hard outer covering of a tree trunk

**crowd out** *phr v.* to push or force someone or something out of an area

**dangle** *v.* to hang loosely, often while swinging back and forth

**gather** *v.* to collect

**germinate** *v.* to start to grow or develop

**get rid of** *phr v.* to remove; to eliminate

**ideal** *adj.* perfect; very good

**invasive species** *n.* any species that is not native to the area in which it is living

**monumental** *adv.* enormous; huge; very large

**ornamental** *adj.* decorative; used as a decoration

**particularly** *adv.* especially; very

**pod** *n.* a long case in which there are seeds

**resprout** *v.* to start growing again

**soil** *n.* dirt; earth; ground

**strip** *n.* a long, thin piece of something

**take over** *phr v.* to take control over; to control completely

**task** *n.* a job; a chore; work to be done

**tendency** *n.* a natural inclination or leaning to act in a certain way

**viable** *adj.* capable of living

## Chapter 07

**assume** *v.* to take for granted; to suppose

**attractive** *adj.* having the power to please or draw interest

**boost** *v.* to make higher or greater; to increase

**contract** *n.* an agreement, particularly one that is written

**cycle** *n.* a set of events that keep coming back in the same order

**efficiency** *n.* the amount of work needed to produce something

**factor** *n.* a cause that brings about a result

**flat** *adj.* unchanging; fixed

**fluctuate** *v.* to rise and fall; to change continually

**forgo** *v.* to do without; to let go of something

**guarantee** *v.* to make certain

**incentive** *n.* something that causes a person to act in a certain way

**productivity** *n.* the amount of work a person does

**reward** *v.* to give something in return, especially for good work or a good deed

**skeptical** *adj.* having or showing doubt; disbelieving

**stability** *n.* the state of being unchanging

**staff** *n.* workers; employees

**steady** *adj.* without change; continuing

**suited** *adj.* meant or adapted for an occasion or use; appropriate

**virtually** *adv.* almost but not quite; nearly; practically

**anonymous**  *adj.* without a known name

**application**  *n.* a way of being used

**deal with**  *phr v.* to do business with someone

**despise**  *v.* to dislike strongly; to scorn

**hinder**  *v.* to be or get in the way of; to obstruct

**impersonal**  *adj.* feeling or showing no strong emotional involvement

**in conjunction with**  *prep.* together with

**insignificant**  *adj.* not important; of no consequence

**interactive**  *adj.* acting or capable of acting on each other or together

**moderate**  *adj.* being within reasonable limits; not extreme

**navigate**  *v.* to move through the menu arrangement in a software program

**previous**  *adj.* happening before in time or order

**recognize**  *v.* to remember the identity of a person or thing

**representative**  *n.* an individual who speaks or acts in place of others

**screen**  *v.* to separate a group into smaller parts

**segment**  *v.* to make several different parts in order

**series**  *n.* a number of things placed or occurring one after the other

**survey**  *n.* a gathering of a sample of data or opinions considered to be representative of a whole

# MEMO

**MEMO**

# MEMO

# TOEFL® MAP Writing

## New TOEFL® Edition

Intermediate

# Scripts and Answer Key

 **DARAKWON**

# TOEFL® MAP Writing

**New TOEFL® Edition**

Intermediate

## Scripts and Answer Key

 **DARAKWON**

▶ Introduction | 01 **Writing Section**

## Information Organization Exercise      p.13

Answers may vary.

1 • **Thesis statement** *Children should only play sports for fun.*

  • **First Supporting Argument** *Playing competitive sports can stress children out.*

    **Detailed Supporting Example** *Children are more sensitive than adults.*

  • **Second Supporting Argument** *Playing to win can make children too aggressive.*

    **Detailed Supporting Example** *Children who play competitive sports are usually more violent.*

  • **Third Supporting Argument** *Children just want to have fun with their friends.*

    **Detailed Supporting Example** *Most children do not care about winning or losing.*

2 • **Thesis Statement** *Learning another language has many benefits.*

  • **First Supporting Argument** *Understanding a foreign language makes it easier to communicate with more people.*

    **Detailed Supporting Example** *By learning Spanish, you can communicate with 570 million people.*

  • **Second Supporting Argument** *Studying a foreign language also makes you smarter.*

    **Detailed Supporting Example** *It helps develop parts of the brain related to speech.*

  • **Third Supporting Argument** *Speaking a second language can help you get a job.*

    **Detailed Supporting Example** *Knowing a second language shows employers that you are hard working.*

▶ Introduction | 02 **Integrated Writing Section**

## Paraphrasing and Summarizing      p.18

❁ **Sample Paraphrasing and Summarizing Exercise**

**Paraphrasing Exercise**

1 Both humans and *the ecosystem* can be *negatively affected* by GM crops.

2 GM crops can *give their traits* to other plants by fertilizing them *with their pollen*.

3 Only *wealthy farmers* can purchase GM crops even though they were made *to help poor farmers*.

4 Numerous countries *do not allow* the growth and sale of *genetically modified foods* for safety reasons.

**Summarizing Exercise**

In the lecture, the professor questions *the value of GMOs* as a means to solve world hunger. His first argument explains how GM crops can *damage the environment* by spreading their traits to other plant species. His next point is about the high costs of GMO farming technology. Even though these crops were developed to help poor farmers, they are *too expensive* for these people to purchase. This negates the benefits of increased crop production of GMOs. The instructor concludes his lecture by *criticizing the safety* of GM crops. He explains that because they *cause health problems*, these crops have been banned in numerous countries.

## Tandem Note-Taking      p.20

Answers may vary.

| Reading | Listening |
| --- | --- |
| **Main Idea** | **Main Idea** |
| GMOs are the best solution for ending world hunger. | GM crops pose a risk to both people and the environment. |
| **First Supporting Argument** | **First Supporting Argument** |
| GM foods are resistant to insect pests. | GMOs can cause damage to environment. |
| Supporting Detail | Supporting Detail |
| insecticides not needed; protects environment | GM crops spread traits; superweeds |
| **Second Supporting Argument** | **Second Supporting Argument** |
| These crops produce more crops. | GMO crops and technology are too expensive. |
| Supporting Detail | Supporting Detail |
| 200 bushels of corn, not 120; can save poor farmers | poor farmers cannot afford |
| **Third Supporting Argument** | **Third Supporting Argument** |
| GMOs can help end world hunger. | Scientists are still not sure of the safety of GMOs. |
| Supporting Detail | Supporting Detail |
| contain more vitamins; golden rice | introduce allergens; banned in many nations |

## Strong Response

p.22

[ d ] The author of the reading passage argues in favor of using genetically modified foods to help solve world hunger. [ c ] The lecturer, on the other hand, does not agree with this viewpoint.

[ b ] The reading passage first explains that GMOs are not vulnerable to insect pests and therefore do not require insecticides. [ a ] Meanwhile, the professor contends that genetically modified crops can harm the environment by spreading their traits to other plants. [ e ] He illustrates this point by explaining that this process has resulted in superweeds that cannot be killed by herbicides, which has forced farmers to go back to traditional crops.

[ b ] Next, the reading passage states that GM crops produce more food per acre than regular crops. [ a ] This argument is countered by the instructor. [ e ] He posits that because GMO crops and technology are so expensive, farmers from developing nations cannot afford them. This, the professor believes, offsets the benefits of increased crop production from GMOs.

[ b ] The last point made by the reading passage is that GM foods are healthier than traditional foods. [ e ] The example given is golden rice, which contains high amounts of vitamin A. [ a ] The lecturer, on the other hand, questions the safety of GMOs. He believes that they introduce new allergens into foods and add to the spread of antibiotic resistance. This is why many nations have banned the growth and sale of genetically modified foods.

## Weak Response

p.23

**Analysis Exercise**

1 (B)

Answer (B) is the best choice because it more accurately summarizes the information from the reading passage. Answer (A) misrepresents the information in the passage while Answer (C) is too general.

2 (A)

Answer (A) is the best choice because this sentence explains why GMOs are unhealthy, which is mentioned in the previous sentence.

---

Introduction | **03** Independent Writing Section

## Generating Ideas

p.27

Answers may vary.

**Idea Box** **Agree**

1 *In the past, very few people were well educated or attended college.*

2 *People today need more skills than in the past. These include computer skills.*

3 *It has become more limiting over time. Now only rich people are considered successful.*

**Reason 1:** *There was less competition.*

**Reason 2:** *Workers did not need to master as many skills in the past.*

**Reason 3:** *People's ideas of success have changed over time.*

**Idea Box** **Disagree**

1 *At that time, many people worked long hours at difficult jobs. Few people had easy jobs.*

2 *Most people had limited opportunities for success. Few people could afford a good education.*

3 *At that time, the most successful people were the wealthy and the naturally talented.*

**Reason 1:** *More people in the past were harder working.*

**Reason 2:** *There were fewer opportunities to be successful.*

**Reason 3:** *Only naturally talented middle-class people could be successful.*

## Outlining Exercise

p.28

Answers may vary.

| Agree | Disagree |
| --- | --- |
| **Thesis Statement** | **Thesis Statement** |
| *I wholeheartedly agree that it was easier to be successful in the past.* | *I believe that it is easier to be successful today than it was in times before.* |
| **First Supporting Idea** | **First Supporting Idea** |
| *There was less competition.* | *More people in the past were harder working.* |
| Supporting Example | Supporting Example |
| *fewer educated people* | *everybody worked long hours; difficult jobs* |

| | |
|---|---|
| **Second Supporting Idea** | **Second Supporting Idea** |
| *Workers did not need to master as many skills in the past.* | *There were fewer opportunities to be successful.* |
| Supporting Example | Supporting Example |
| *only understand trade; today, need many skills* | *only rich were educated* |
| **Third Supporting Idea** | **Third Supporting Idea** |
| *People's ideas of success have changed over time.* | *Only naturally talented middle-class people could be successful.* |
| Supporting Example | Supporting Example |
| *in past, owning home was successful; today must be rich* | *Beethoven; had natural talent* |
| **Conclusion** | **Conclusion** |
| *For the reasons given above, I agree that it was easier to be successful in the past.* | *Ultimately, I contend that it is easier for most people to be successful today.* |

## Strong Response

p.30

[ d ] I disagree that it was easier to be successful in the past than it is today for three reasons. [ b ] First, in previous times working hard was necessary just to get by. Second, there were fewer opportunities for average people to excel. Finally, the people who were successful in the past were highly gifted and diligent.

[ f ] To begin with, most people in the past needed to work hard in order to survive. [ c ] They worked long hours at difficult jobs. [ e ] To be more specific, it was common to work sixty hours or more per week at physically difficult jobs. Therefore, people had little time or energy to do more than what was required of them. Today, many people work in office jobs for only forty hours per week. Because they have more free time and energy, they are able to do extra work to get ahead. In this way, it is easier for employees today to stand out.

[ f ] Another factor that made it difficult to be successful in the past was that there were fewer opportunities for people to get ahead. [ c ] For centuries, the vast majority of people learned a trade from a young age or worked on their families' farms. They could not easily do something different or unique. [ e ] This is illustrated by the fact that most successful people in the past were born into royal or rich families. These privileged members of society received the best educations and had many opportunities to succeed. In contrast, unlike today, the majority of average people did not have these opportunities given to them.

[ f ] On top of this, middle-class people who were successful in the past were very gifted. [ c ] Back then, only people with natural talent could stand out from the common people. [ e ] For example, consider the case of Ludwig van Beethoven. His musical ability was evident from an early age, and he was able to develop his skill on his own. If he had not been born with his talent, he might have never become successful. Today, however, average people can compensate for their lack of natural ability by going to college and gaining certification.

[ a ] Ultimately, I contend that it is easier for more people to be successful today. [ g ] Thanks to increased wealth and educational opportunities, average people can now excel beyond the norm and achieve success.

## Weak Response

p.31

**Q Analysis Exercise**

**Q**

Answer Ⓒ is the best choice because it most clearly supports the main idea of the response. Answer Ⓐ does not relate directly to the topic while Answer Ⓑ contradicts the main thesis of the response.

Chapter | **01** Integrated Writing

Zoology: **Bonobos and Chimpanzees**

**Reading**                                           p.34

| **Paraphrasing** |

1 Scientists have found that bonobos and chimpanzees *behave differently* when they are *being kept in zoos*.

2 Unlike chimpanzees, which are *violent animals*, bonobos are *peaceful animals*.

3 Bonobos are not *violent toward one another* even when they have arguments.

4 Chimpanzees rely on *violent behavior* in order to *solve their disagreements*.

| **Summarizing** |

The reading passage mainly deals with the differences in behavior *between bonobos and chimpanzees*. The passage gives two supporting ideas to support this claim. First, the passage explains that chimpanzees act *much more aggressively* when they are being kept in zoos. The example given that illustrates this idea is the fact that bonobos *cooperate with researchers* while chimpanzees do not. Second, the passage talks about how *bonobos are more peaceful* animals than chimpanzees. The passage shows this by explaining that chimpanzees *rely on violence* whereas bonobos do not.

**Listening**                                          p.36

**Script** 02-01

**Professor:** I would like to finish my lecture today by talking about our primate cousins, the chimpanzee and the bonobo. According to many studies, these animals have very different personalities from one another. But it turns out that there are other explanations for the actions of the so-called aggressive chimp and the peaceful bonobo.

For one thing, animals behave differently depending on the situation. What I mean is that just because an animal reacts a certain way in one situation does not mean that it will react the same way in another situation. So how does this relate to the findings about bonobos and chimps? Well, think about it. Studies of bonobos have shown them to be

less aggressive than chimps. But this is only when they are both in captivity. Therefore, the way the animals act in zoos does not illustrate how they act when they are in their natural surroundings. In other words, these experiments are invalid because they don't compare how bonobos and chimps act in the wild.

Here's another thing to consider. Bonobos may not live such harmonious lives after all. You see, for a long time, zoologists thought that bonobos lived in peace and avoided direct conflict. But researchers recently made a shocking discovery. They found that smaller bonobos actually attack larger ones. The reason that researchers had not discovered this sooner is that the smaller bonobos only attack when there are no other creatures around. This discovery suggests that bonobos are not the tranquil animals they were once thought to be.

| **Paraphrasing** |

1 Research done on bonobos in captivity has shown them to be *more peaceful* than chimpanzees.

2 Because they do not compare the way bonobos and chimpanzees act *in different environments*, these studies are not valid.

3 Zoologists long believed that bonobos were *peaceful creatures* that did not *fight with one another*.

4 Scientists only recently learned about this because *the small bonobos* only attack when they are alone *with a larger bonobo*.

| **Summarizing** |

The professor's lecture explains that bonobos may not be as peaceful as *commonly believed*. She gives two supporting ideas to support her thesis. First, she mentions that *animals behave differently* according to *their situations*. She explains that because studies of bonobos and chimpanzees have only observed *their behavior in captivity*, they are not valid. Second, she talks about how bonobos interact with one another by saying that *they are not as peaceful as* previously thought. To explain this idea, the professor talks about new research which has found that smaller bonobos *attack larger bonobos* when they are *alone together*.

Answers may vary.

| Reading | Listening |
|---|---|
| **Main Idea**<br><br>*Bonobos are usually peaceful, but chimpanzees are more violent.* | **Main Idea**<br><br>*There might be other explanations for why bonobos seem to be peaceful and chimpanzees aggressive.* |
| **First Supporting Argument**<br><br>*When they are in captivity, bonobos are calm and relaxed, but chimpanzees act much more aggressively.* | **First Supporting Argument**<br><br>*Animals behave differently depending on the situation.* |
| Supporting Detail<br><br>*bonobos playful and cooperative; chimpanzees uncooperative; break equipment* | Supporting Detail<br><br>*studies only compare behavior in captivity; need to study them in natural surroundings* |
| **Second Supporting Argument**<br><br>*Bonobos live in peace and harmony while chimpanzees resort to physical violence.* | **Second Supporting Argument**<br><br>*Bonobos may not live in harmony with one another.* |
| Supporting Detail<br><br>*bonobos don't fight with one another; larger chimpanzees attack smaller ones* | Supporting Detail<br><br>*smaller bonobos attack larger ones* |

**Strong Response**  p.40

| Critical Analysis |

1   The reading passage suggests that bonobos are much more peaceful than chimpanzees, but the professor's lecture casts doubt on this claim. / The instructor begins her lecture by explaining that animals change the way they act to adapt to their situations. / Next, the lecturer talks about how bonobos may not live in total harmony with one another.

2   She talks about how this relates to studies of bonobos and chimpanzees. / Because these studies only focused on animals in captivity, they are invalid since they do not explain how bonobos and chimpanzees act in the wild. / She says that zoologists had believed that bonobos were peaceful animals. / However, they have recently discovered that smaller bonobos actually attack larger bonobos. / Scientists did not learn about this sooner because the smaller bonobos only attack where there is no one around.

3   invalid

4   It means to live with social agreement. The sentence that explains this idea is: However, they have recently discovered that smaller bonobos actually attack larger bonobos.

5   The instructor begins her lecture by explaining… / Next, the lecturer talks about… / However…

**Weak Response**  p.41

| Critical Analysis |

1   Ⓑ

Answer Ⓑ is the best choice because it best explains the ideas of the reading passage and the lecture.

2   Ⓑ

Answer Ⓑ is the best choice because the previous sentence describes bonobo behavior while the sentence after it notes that the animals are different in this way.

3   The lecture that followed the reading passage brought up many counterarguments. / First, the passage said that bonobos are much calmer than chimpanzees. / She said that because these studies have only examined animals in captivity, they are invalid. / Next, the reading passage argues that bonobos are much more peaceful than chimpanzees.

▶ Chapter | **01** Independent Writing

**Teachers Should Update Their Knowledge Regularly**

**Generating Ideas**  p.42

Idea Box   Agree

1   *New teaching methods are developed all the time. Teachers need to know about them.*

2   *Students benefit by having teachers who know how to teach effectively. Schools benefit by having teachers who can help students do their best work.*

3   *Some other jobs include doctor, lawyer, computer programmer, and scientist.*

**Reason 1:** *Teachers need to be aware of the latest teaching methods.*

**Reason 2:** *People with more training are able to do their jobs better.*

1   Teachers learn something new and improve their teaching skills every time they teach.

2   Teachers need to get degrees in education and certification from their state.

3   The new methods teachers learn may not be tested or effective in practice.

**Reason 1:** Teachers are already certified experts.

**Reason 2:** Teachers receive feedback on a daily basis.

## Planning

p.43

Answers may vary.

| Agree | Disagree |
|---|---|
| **Thesis Statement**<br>I believe that teachers should be required to update their knowledge every five years. | **Thesis Statement**<br>I believe that teachers are capable of improving their abilities on their own. |
| **First Supporting Idea**<br>Teachers need to be aware of the latest teaching methods. | **First Supporting Idea**<br>Teachers are already certified experts. |
| Supporting Example<br>more effective ways to teach concepts; using computers in the classroom | Supporting Example<br>have education degrees; get certification |
| **Second Supporting Idea**<br>People with more training are able to do their jobs better. | **Second Supporting Idea**<br>Teachers receive feedback on a daily basis. |
| Supporting Example<br>students with higher test scores | Supporting Example<br>feedback from students, parents, and teachers; helps teachers improve |
| **Conclusion**<br>Teachers must be required to update their knowledge. | **Conclusion**<br>It is clear that teachers should not be required to update their knowledge. |

## Strong Response

p.45

| Critical Analysis |

1   I disagree that teachers need to update their knowledge every five years for two reasons. / First of all, teachers are already certified experts. / In addition, teachers receive feedback on a daily basis. / It is clear that teachers should not be required to update their knowledge because they already do so

by themselves.

2   In university education programs, potential teachers are taught how to create lesson plans, how to motivate students, and how to teach effectively. / Once they graduate, these students have to pass state certification tests in order to obtain their teaching licenses. / Passing these exams requires students to have a deep understanding of the subject they want to teach as well as various teaching methods to use in the classroom. / For instance, my older sister is a teacher. / During her first year of teaching, many of her students were not doing well in her classes. / My sister was not sure about what to do, so she got some advice from the older, more experienced teachers at her school. / As a result, her students' performances increased dramatically. / Today, she is one of her school's top teachers.

3   how a college student becomes a teacher / the situation of the older sister who is a teacher

## Weak Response

p.46

| Critical Analysis |

1   Ⓒ

Answer Ⓒ is the best choice because it explains the main idea of the essay clearly. Answer Ⓐ is not clear enough to be used while Answer Ⓑ goes against the main idea of the essay.

2   First, an instructor's teaching methods can become outdated over time.

3   [Give an example of a teacher from school who used old techniques and how this teacher's lessons were less effective as a result.]

4   They think that teachers are not as good as they should be. / Most teachers graduated from university a long time ago, so their knowledge is outdated. / Some teachers believe that they do not need to update their knowledge because they already know about teaching.

History: **The Collapse of Egypt's Old Kingdom**

**Reading**                                                        p.48

| Paraphrasing |

1   The power of the pharaohs and royal families was *unchallenged during most* of the Old Kingdom.

2   Local governors *began to question* the power of the central government.

3   Evidence shows that a drought *lasting half a century* occurred in Egypt at this time.

4   A lack of food resulted in *deaths and rebellions* by citizens around the nation.

| Summarizing |

The reading passage focuses on the events that caused *the downfall* of Egypt's Old Kingdom. The passage includes two supporting arguments to explain this. First, the passage states that the central government's *loss of power* contributed to the collapse. This is supported by the example of the regional governors who *challenged the rule* of the pharaoh. Second, the passage explains that *a major drought* also brought down *the Old Kingdom*. This is illustrated by the fact that many peasant revolts occurred as a result of *food shortages* caused by *the lack of rainfall*.

**Listening**                                                      p.50

Script   02-02

**Professor:** Let's start our discussion today by talking about the events that occurred during the last part of the Old Kingdom. Some believe that the Old Kingdom collapsed due to widespread conflict and destabilization. However, I'm not so sure that this was really the case. Let me give you a couple of examples to show you why I feel this way.

Near the end of the Old Kingdom, the central government had lost some of its power. But this does not mean that it had no influence beyond the capital. The pharaohs recognized the importance of maintaining connections between regional leaders and the royal family. So the central government would present special rewards to governors who remained loyal. Moreover, the pharaohs commanded strong central armies. As a result, any uprisings were quickly put down. Thus, there were no advantages for governors to stage revolts against the pharaohs.

And then there's the common belief that a famine occurred during the final years of the Old Kingdom. This idea is based on a historical document that contains records of a tremendous decrease in rainfall throughout Egypt during that time. It turns out, though, that this document was not made in Egypt at all. It was actually from a region to the east. Although this region was adjacent to Egypt, the weather in the two places was completely different. Therefore, we cannot conclude that the Old Kingdom experienced famine and drought based solely on this document.

| Paraphrasing |

1   The pharaohs understood that it was important to maintain a relationship between *local leaders and the royal family*.

2   *Therefore*, local leaders would not *gain anything by challenging* the central government.

3   Many people also think that *a drought* happened during *the late Old Kingdom*.

4   The climate in this area was *totally dissimilar* even though the two places were located *next to each other*.

| Summarizing |

The lecturer calls into question the arguments *made in the reading passage*. He offers two pieces of evidence to support his viewpoint. First, he explains that regional governors had little reason to *challenge the pharaoh's rule*. He believes this because the pharaoh *would reward loyal governors* and was in command of *a powerful army*. Second, the instructor states that there may not have actually been *a drought during the Old Kingdom*. He claims that the historical document describing the drought is from another region, which means that it is impossible to conclude that *there was a drought in Egypt*.

**Tandem Note-Taking**                                             p.52

Answers may vary.

| Reading | Listening |
| --- | --- |
| **Main Idea** | **Main Idea** |
| *A series of terrible events led to the collapse of the Old Kingdom in Egypt.* | *The Old Kingdom may not have collapsed for these reasons.* |
| **First Supporting Argument** | **First Supporting Argument** |
| *The central government became weaker.* | *The central government was still powerful and influential.* |

*regional governors greedy; challenged the pharaoh; civil wars*

**Second Supporting Argument**

*Egypt suffered a severe drought for many years.*

Supporting Detail

*could not water crops; were many deaths; were peasant revolts*

Supporting Detail

*rewarded loyal governors; used army to stop uprisings*

**Second Supporting Argument**

*There may not have been a drought in Egypt.*

Supporting Detail

*document not from Egypt; cannot know if drought occurred*

---

**Strong Response**                                     p.54

| Critical Analysis |

1   The reading passage's author is convinced that a series of terrible events resulted in the collapse of Egypt's Old Kingdom, yet the lecturer disagrees that this was the main reason for its downfall. / The first reason that the reading passage gives for the downfall of the Old Kingdom is the weakening of Egypt's central government. / The reading passage's author also believes that a severe drought contributed to the fall of the Old Kingdom.

2   Meanwhile, the professor explains that the pharaohs were still influential even though they had lost some of their power. / He concludes that these leaders would not have gained anything by challenging the rule of the pharaohs. / He explains that the historical document about the drought was not written in Egypt. / However, the lecturer explains that the historical document about the drought was not written in Egypt but was instead from a region east of Egypt that had completely different weather. / This means that there is no evidence to support the claim that the Old Kingdom collapsed because of a severe drought.

3   challenging

4   It means a long period of no rain. The sentence that explains this is: The reason is that the lack of rainfall led to widespread food shortages and peasant revolts.

5   The first reason the reading passage gives is… / Meanwhile… / The reading passage's author also believes… / However…

---

**Weak Response**                                       p.55

| Critical Analysis |

1   Ⓑ

    Answer Ⓑ is the best choice because it correctly explains the information from the reading. Answers Ⓐ and Ⓒ are incorrect because they misrepresent information in the passage.

2   Ⓐ

    Answer Ⓐ is the best choice because the sentence serves as a transition between the information from the lecture and the reading passage.

3   The reading passage mainly deals with the collapse of the Old Kingdom in Egypt. / The reading passage begins by explaining that the weakening of the central government contributed to the collapse. / The professor says that the pharaoh would reward governors for being loyal and that the pharaoh controlled a strong army. / It explains that farmers relied on floodwaters from the Nile to irrigate their crops, but the drought prevented the flooding from occurring.

---

Chapter | **02** Independent Writing

**Sometimes It Is Better Not to Say Anything**

**Generating Ideas**                                    p.56

**Idea Box** **Agree**

1   *Saying things that are not nice usually makes people angry and upset.*

2   *When people do not know about their problems, they are likely to be happier than if they are told about their shortcomings.*

3   *You should never say something critical when you are talking to a very sensitive person, when you are dealing with an impatient supervisor, or when you are not trying to be helpful.*

**Reason 1:** *Saying things that are not nice can unnecessarily hurt a person's feelings.*

**Reason 2:** *There are times when being critical can make a situation worse for many people.*

**Idea Box** **Disagree**

1   *Saying things that are not nice can make people understand and fix their problems.*

2   *If people do not know about their problems,
    then they can never improve themselves. This
    is a concern, especially if a person has serious
    problems.*

3   *You should say something critical when you know
    a person well, are talking with that person privately,
    and are as nice and constructive as possible with
    your criticism.*

**Reason 1:** *Being critical can help a person correct
personal shortcomings.*

**Reason 2:** *Saying something that is not nice can help
make bad situations better.*

**Planning**                                                   p.57

Answers may vary.

| Agree | Disagree |
|---|---|
| **Thesis Statement** | **Thesis Statement** |
| *I feel that if you cannot say anything nice, then it is better not to say anything at all.* | *I believe that saying something that is a bit mean or critical is sometimes beneficial.* |
| **First Supporting Idea** | **First Supporting Idea** |
| *Saying things that are not nice can unnecessarily hurt a person's feelings.* | *Being critical can help a person correct personal shortcomings.* |
| **Supporting Example** | **Supporting Example** |
| *overweight friend; became very sad and angry* | *friend says rude things; does not realize this* |
| **Second Supporting Idea** | **Second Supporting Idea** |
| *There are times when being critical can make a situation worse for many people.* | *Saying something that is not nice can help make bad situations better.* |
| **Supporting Example** | **Supporting Example** |
| *telling a manager about his bad breath; punished everybody* | *friend too sensitive; help make him thick skinned* |
| **Conclusion** | **Conclusion** |
| *I contend that most of the time, it is better not to say anything at all if you cannot say something nice.* | *Although some might disagree, I firmly believe that there are times when it is better to say something that is not nice.* |

**Strong Response**                                            p.59

| **Critical Analysis** |

1   As for me, I still believe that if you can't say anything
    nice, it is better not to say anything at all. / To begin
    with, people often say mean things that are not

constructive and only hurt the feelings of others. /
There are also times when saying something critical
can worsen a situation for everyone involved. /
In conclusion, I contend that there are certain
situations when it is better not to tell the truth.

2   When I was in high school, I had a friend who was
    severely overweight. / Although her weight problem
    was obvious, my friend was in denial about it. /
    One day, she asked me if I thought she was getting
    too heavy. / I told her that she was too fat and that
    she should lose about twenty kilograms. / She
    immediately began crying and ran away from me. /
    After that, she never spoke to me again. / This was
    the case at one of my part-time summer jobs. / The
    manager at my store had a serious case of bad
    breath, but nobody was brave enough to tell him. /
    Eventually, one of my co-workers told the manager
    about his problem. / Even though my co-worker was
    trying to be helpful, the manager became furious. /
    He made everybody do extra work for the rest of the
    month and was very mean to all of us. / If none of
    us had said anything, this situation would not have
    happened.

3   telling an overweight friend about her weight
    problem / telling a manager about his bad breath

**Weak Response**                                              p.60

| **Critical Analysis** |

1   Ⓐ

    Answer Ⓐ is the best choice because the first body
    paragraph is mainly about how help others improve
    themselves.

2   Another reason I believe this is that saying
    something that is not nice can improve a situation.

3   [Explain how telling a friend about her rude behavior
    helped her improve her attitude.]

4   However, I feel that hiding your true feelings from
    somebody creates more problems than just being
    honest with that person. / One reason that I believe
    honest comments are sometimes necessary is
    that they can help others improve themselves.
    / We are best able to make corrections to our
    appearance or behavior when people tell us about
    our shortcomings. / Another reason I believe this
    is that saying something that is not nice can help a
    person become stronger. / Some people will tell you
    that if you cannot say anything nice, it is better to
    say nothing at all.

Biology: **Yawning Lowers Blood Temperature**

**Reading**                                                    p.62

| Paraphrasing |

1   The brain's oxygen levels *can decrease a lot* when we *are not doing anything*.

2   By yawning, people are *able to stay focused* by bringing in *oxygen* and getting rid of *carbon dioxide* in the brain.

3   According to the study, test scores of *students who yawned* were *five percent higher* than those who did not yawn.

4   When people yawn, they move *the lower-temperature blood* from other parts of their bodies to *their brains*.

| Summarizing |

The main topic of the reading passage is *the purpose of yawning*. The author presents two supporting theories. The first is that yawning helps *increase the brain's oxygen levels*. According to the example, yawning helps students perform better on tests. The next argument is that yawning *cools the brain*. The passage states that people bring *cooler blood into their brains* when they yawn. In turn, this helps them concentrate more easily.

**Listening**                                                 p.64

**Script** 02-03

**Professor:** You may be thinking that the mystery behind yawning has been solved. It's true that there are some convincing theories as to what causes yawning, including one argument that claims that yawning improves brain performance. But let me assure you that none of these claims stands up to further examination.

First, there is the argument that yawning occurs as a result of low oxygen levels in the brain. However, new studies have suggested otherwise. Scientists have conducted experiments to determine whether changes in oxygen levels cause people to yawn. They tested this in a couple of different ways. In one test, the scientists put some subjects in a room with increased oxygen levels. In another test, they decreased the carbon dioxide levels. What they found was that the frequency of yawning by the participants did not change at all. So what did this

mean? It suggested that oxygen levels in the brain have nothing to do with yawning.

There is also the belief that yawning cools the brain. If this were true, then people would yawn more often on hot days. But does this really happen? Well, one group of researchers found out. They first determined the number of times most people yawn on average. The researchers then compared this data with how often people yawned on warmer days. And what was the result? They found that even in hot weather, people do not yawn more often. From these results, we can conclude that yawning does little to regulate the brain's temperature.

| Paraphrasing |

1   Researchers have performed studies *to figure out if yawning* is caused by differences in *oxygen levels*.

2   They discovered that *the number of times* participants yawned *remained the same*.

3   The scientists began by calculating *how often people usually* yawn.

4   Based on these findings, it is safe to say that *the brain's temperature* is not affected by yawning.

| Summarizing |

In the lecture, the professor argues that the *purpose of yawning* is still not understood. To explain this, she gives two reasons. The instructor mentions that yawning does not seem to affect *the brain's oxygen levels*. Scientists found that *changing the oxygen and carbon dioxide* levels did not cause people to yawn more or less often. The lecturer moves on to discuss how yawning can *lower blood temperature*. According to a study, people do not *yawn more frequently* on hot days. This suggests that the brain's temperature is not affected by yawning.

**Tandem Note-Taking**                                        p.66

Answers may vary.

| Reading | Listening |
| --- | --- |
| **Main Idea** | **Main Idea** |
| *Thanks to recent discoveries, scientists may have discovered the reasons behind yawning.* | *None of the claims about the causes of yawning stands up to further examination.* |
| **First Supporting Argument** | **First Supporting Argument** |
| *One cause for a person to yawn deals with oxygen levels.* | *According to recent studies, oxygen levels do not relate to yawning.* |

| Supporting Detail | Supporting Detail |
|---|---|
| *yawning students; higher test scores* | *changing oxygen levels; not yawning more* |
| **Second Supporting Argument** | **Second Supporting Argument** |
| *Another purpose of yawning is that it helps lower the brain's blood temperature.* | *Furthermore, yawning may not lower the brain's temperature.* |
| Supporting Detail | Supporting Detail |
| *yawn when concentrating* | *don't yawn more on hot days* |

**Strong Response**　　　　　　　　p.68

| **Critical Analysis** |

1　The reading passage argues that yawning controls brain activity, but the arguments presented by the lecturer call these findings into question. / First, the professor states that yawning does not affect the brain's oxygen levels. / The instructor then goes on to argue that yawning does not affect the brain's temperature.

2　She mentions an experiment during which scientists placed subjects in a room and changed the levels of oxygen and carbon dioxide. / The researchers discovered that the number of times the subjects yawned did not change. / This implied that low oxygen levels do not cause yawning. / She talks about an experiment that measured the number of times people yawn on normal days and on hot days. / The scientists found that people do not yawn more often when the weather is warmer. / This suggests that temperature changes do not cause people to yawn.

3　increase

4　It means to go against something. The sentence that explains this is: This contradicts the idea that yawning helps cool the brain, which is the argument presented in the reading passage.

5　First… / The instructor then goes on to argue…

**Weak Response**　　　　　　　　p.69

1　Ⓒ

　　Answer Ⓒ is the best choice because it correctly summarizes the information from the sentences. Answers Ⓐ and Ⓑ are incorrect because they misrepresent information in the sentences.

2　Ⓐ

　　Answer Ⓐ is the best choice because it contradicts

the sentence coming before it that suggests that we yawn when our brains get too warm.

3　The reading passage provides some theories about the causes of yawning, but the professor calls these into question. / The reading passage begins by saying that yawning lowers oxygen levels in the brain. / In conclusion, the author of the reading passage believes that yawning is beneficial for the brain while the professor remains unsure.

◗ Chapter | **03 Independent Writing**

**Looks Are More Important than Ideas**

**Generating Ideas**　　　　　　　　p.70

**Idea Box** Agree

1　*People may think an attractive person is smarter than a person who is less attractive.*

2　*Those who are more attractive are probably treated better. The reason is that people want to be liked by good-looking people.*

3　*Some of those jobs include being a spokesperson, singer, actor, and salesperson.*

**Reason 1:** *Our society values attractiveness very much.*

**Reason 2:** *People who are more attractive get treated better and make more money.*

**Idea Box** Disagree

1　*When somebody is too attractive, other people may feel jealous and angry.*

2　*Jobs where good ideas are more important are scientist, businessperson, inventor, teacher, and analyst.*

3　*Some very successful include Bill Gates and Warren Buffet. They are average looking.*

**Reason 1:** *Good ideas are more important than good looks in the long term.*

**Reason 2:** *Being too attractive can make other people feel jealous.*

p.71

Answers may vary.

| Agree | Disagree |
|---|---|
| **Thesis Statement** | **Thesis Statement** |
| *I agree that good looks are more important than good ideas.* | *Although looking good is important, I feel that having good ideas is more important.* |
| **First Supporting Idea** | **First Supporting Idea** |
| *Our society values attractiveness very much.* | *Good ideas are more important than good looks in the long term.* |
| Supporting Example | Supporting Example |
| *ads with attractive people; judge others based on looks* | *need ideas for success in business* |
| **Second Supporting Idea** | **Second Supporting Idea** |
| *People who are more attractive get treated better and make more money.* | *Being too attractive can make other people feel jealous.* |
| Supporting Example | Supporting Example |
| *earn ten percent more money* | *very pretty coworker; other females mean to her* |
| **Conclusion** | **Conclusion** |
| *It is clear that being successful requires good looks.* | *Looking good can be beneficial, but having good ideas is even more helpful.* |

p.73

| **Critical Analysis** |

1 Taking this into consideration, it becomes evident that looking good is more important for success than having good ideas. / One reason that looking good is so critical for success is that our society values attractiveness so much. / Even after we have made our first impression, being attractive remains important. / In summary, it is clear that being successful requires good looks.

2 In magazines and on television, you see only the most attractive people and the good things they do. / At the same time, you see advertisements for fashion, weight-loss programs, and plastic surgery. / These services exist because people want to look their best. / They feel this way for good reason. / According to research, people formulate opinions of others based solely on their looks. / We make inferences about people's intelligence, educational attainment, and personality based on their appearance. / To give an example, recent surveys have found that people who are tall, thin, and attractive earn nearly ten percent more than those who are average looking. / In fields where looks are

important, the income gap is even greater. / On top of this, the study found that people who look below average earn fifteen percent less money than people of average attractiveness.

3 advertisements for fashion, weight loss, and plastic surgery / good-looking people earn more money

p.74

| **Critical Analysis** |

1 Ⓒ

Answer Ⓒ is the best choice because it most clearly supports the main idea of the essay. Answer Ⓐ is too general, and Answer Ⓑ goes against the thesis of the response.

2 Finally, some of the most successful people are not especially handsome.

3 [Give an example of a female coworker who was much prettier than all the other female employees. Explain how the other female employees treated her badly.]

4 Some people may agree with this statement, but I feel that good ideas are more important for success than good looks. / These jobs do not require good-looking employees but, rather, ones with good ideas. / Another reason I feel this way is that looking good sometimes causes other people to feel jealous. / Consider people like Bill Gates and Warren Buffet, who are successful because of their ideas, not their looks.

Chapter | 04 Integrated Writing

Education: **Higher Education Should Be Free**

p.76

| **Paraphrasing** |

1 *Wealthy nations* today must provide their people *with a higher education*.

2 As result, a lot of *talented students* cannot afford *a college education*.

3 Research shows that educated people more often donate *their time and money* to their communities.

4 Higher education must be *made free* in order to *make life better* for everybody.

The topic of the reading passage is *making higher education free*. The first reason the author gives is that wealthy nations must educate their citizens *to stay competitive*. This is illustrated by the fact that most European nations already offer *free higher education* to their citizens. Next, the reading passage states that providing free higher education brings *indirect benefits to communities*. These include greater participation in volunteer events and lower crime rates.

**Listening**                                                    p.78

Script 02-04

**Professor:** As college students, I'm sure one of your main concerns is paying your yearly tuition. No doubt, free higher education sounds like a great idea, right? Well, let's just say there are a few unintended consequences of such a plan. Allow me to explain to you what they are.

One result of tuition-free higher education affects all citizens of a nation. You know what I'm talking about. Yep—higher taxes. You see, if the students aren't paying their own tuition, then the funding for the schools has to come from somewhere. In this case, it comes from taxpayers. In fact, one recent study estimated that in order to provide all students with free higher education, the government would have to raise taxes by more than fifteen percent. The truth is that most Americans simply don't want to spend money on something that doesn't directly benefit them. Because of this, we can safely say that the public will not be willing to provide others with a free college education.

Another less obvious consequence of providing free college educations would be a decrease in the quality of the instruction. The best schools in the country are usually the most expensive. The reason for this is simple. Topnotch professors demand suitably high salaries. If education were made free, then schools could no longer pay these talented instructors enough money. As a result, these educators would simply take their talents elsewhere. Consequently, the value of college educations everywhere would drop. Clearly, a quality higher education must be paid for by the students.

| Paraphrasing |

1    Research shows that taxes would need to be increased by *more than fifteen percent* to pay for free higher education.

2    Therefore, we can conclude that people will not pay for *another person's college education*.

3    A second drawback to *tuition-free higher education* would be a reduction *in the quality of teaching*.

4    By making higher education no cost, universities could not afford to pay *their best professors* high enough salaries.

| Summarizing |

In the lecture, the professor talks about *some potential drawbacks* of free higher education. One of these drawbacks is *paying for free universities*. He explains that taxes would have to be raised by more than fifteen percent. The instructor also says that most Americans would not be willing to pay for something that does not *benefit them directly*. Another drawback the lecturer talks about is the *reduction in the quality* of education. He explains that schools would not be able to *pay the salaries* of their best instructors without charging tuition.

**Tandem Note-Taking**                                           p.80

Answers may vary.

| Reading | Listening |
|---|---|
| **Main Idea** | **Main Idea** |
| *To provide all qualified students with a higher education, American schools must become tuition free.* | *Although free higher education sounds like a great idea, it has some unintended drawbacks.* |
| **First Supporting Argument** | **First Supporting Argument** |
| *Developed nations have a responsibility to educate their citizens.* | *Funding for tuition-free higher education must come from the taxpayers.* |
| Supporting Detail | Supporting Detail |
| *free education in Europe* | *taxes raised by more than fifteen percent* |
| **Second Supporting Argument** | **Second Supporting Argument** |
| *Offering no-cost higher education also indirectly benefits the community.* | *Free higher education would decrease the quality of instruction.* |
| Supporting Detail | Supporting Detail |
| *more educated people donate money and time; lower crime rates* | *schools couldn't pay good professors* |

**Strong Response**

| Critical Analysis |

1 The professor, however, believes that such a plan would have unintended consequences. / To begin with, the reading passage states that developed nations such as the United States have a responsibility to provide their citizens with a free university education. / Next, to rebut the reading passage's argument that free higher education would provide benefits for everyone, the instructor explains how the quality of instruction would be affected. / While the author of the reading passage wants higher education to become free, the professor argues against doing this.

2 However, the lecturer contends that the government would have to raise taxes by more than fifteen percent to pay for free colleges. / He then says that most American people do not want to cover the costs of a service they are not using themselves. / He says that good colleges charge high tuition in order to pay the salaries of professors. / If universities cannot charge tuition, then they cannot pay their best professors enough money to stay. / This would decrease the overall quality of a college education.

3 unintended

4 It means to pay for something. The sentence that explains this is: He then says that most American people do not want to cover the costs of a service they are not using themselves.

5 To begin with… / However… / Next…

**Weak Response**

| Critical Analysis |

1 Ⓐ

Answer Ⓐ is the best choice because it clearly explains the main ideas from the reading passage and the lecture. Answer Ⓑ is incorrect because it confuses the main ideas while Answer Ⓒ is not clear enough.

2 Ⓒ

Answer Ⓒ is the best choice because this sentence gives specific information about the sentence that comes before it.

3 The lecturer's first argument is that making college tuition free would raise taxes. / He contends that most Americans do not want to pay for something that does not benefit them. / If a college education were made free, these schools could no longer

afford to pay their professors enough money. / His argument goes against the one made in the reading passage that making college education free benefits the community.

◗ Chapter | 04 Independent Writing

**Keeping Old Customs or Adopting New Ones**

**Generating Ideas**

**Idea Box** Follow New Customs

1 *It allows a person to understand the culture better, which makes it easier to make friends.*

2 *A person can use local products. This makes a person's life cheaper and more convenient.*

3 *Adopting new customs allows a person to understand how different people think and live.*

**Reason 1:** *Following new customs allows you to live your life differently.*

**Reason 2:** *Adopting the customs of a new country allows you to become part of that culture more easily.*

**Idea Box** Keep Old Customs

1 *By following the customs from home, a person can live life in the way that individual is used to.*

2 *A person may not adopt new customs when they go against the customs of the person's old country.*

3 *Some of these include the language barrier and different ways of thinking.*

**Reason 1:** *Keeping old customs can make your life in a new country more comfortable.*

**Reason 2:** *It is difficult to give up old customs quickly*

**Planning**

Answers may vary.

| Follow New Customs | Keep Old Customs |
| --- | --- |
| **Thesis Statement** | **Thesis Statement** |
| *When you move to a new country, I feel it is better to adopt the customs of that nation.* | *I believe it is better for people to keep their own customs than to adopt those of another country.* |

| First Supporting Idea | First Supporting Idea |
|---|---|
| *Following new customs allows you to live your life differently.* | *Keeping old customs can make your life in a new country more comfortable.* |
| Supporting Example | Supporting Example |
| *eating customs in China* | *eating food from home* |
| **Second Supporting Idea** | **Second Supporting Idea** |
| *Adopting the customs of a new country allows you to become part of that culture more easily.* | *It is difficult to give up old customs quickly.* |
| Supporting Example | Supporting Example |
| *understand culture; make friends easily* | *different language; new culture* |
| **Conclusion** | **Conclusion** |
| *I think it is much better to adopt local customs.* | *It is easier for most people to keep their old customs when they move to a new country.* |

**Strong Response**      p.87

| **Critical Analysis** |

1   When living in a new country, I believe it is essential to adopt the customs of the new country. / One reason to adopt the customs of a new country is that they allow you to live your life differently. / Another reason to adopt new customs is that doing so allows you to assimilate more easily into the local community. / Although some people may prefer to cling to their old ways, for the reasons given above, I think it is much better to adopt local customs.

2   When I was growing up, my family and I lived in China for a couple years. / Many aspects of the culture, such as eating, were very different from those in my home country. / Unlike in my home country, people in China are encouraged to share food. / So while we were in China, we adopted Chinese eating practices and shared our food with one another. / It was foreign to us, but we decided to follow their customs so long as we were living there. / When my wife and I moved to Germany, we were eager to take part in some German festivals. / One of these was Oktoberfest. We went with our neighbors to the city market for the celebration. / We ate great food, played games, and had a lot of fun. More importantly, we made great friends. / This made us feel like welcomed members of the community.

3   different food customs in China / participating in German festivals

**Weak Response**      p.88

| **Critical Analysis** |

1   Ⓐ

Answer Ⓐ is the best choice because it gives an example of why the author's friend kept some customs from his old country.

2   Moreover, it is difficult for people to completely give up their old customs.

3   [Give an example of grandparents who moved to a different country. Explain how and why they kept their old customs.]

4   You understand the way of life in your old country, and this can make it easier to live in your new country. / Most people are willing to try the food from their new country sometimes, but most of the time, they prefer to eat food from their homeland. / It might be possible to adopt the customs of the new country eventually, but most people have to keep their old customs for a while.

**Chapter | 05 Integrated Writing**

Anthropology: **The Purpose of Ancient Roads**

**Reading**      p.90

| **Paraphrasing** |

1   Although archaeologists do not know what the roads *were used for*, they have several ideas.

2   Thus, it is possible that these roads allowed *many people* to *travel between towns*.

3   Researchers contend that these roads were of religious significance based on *their layouts and locations*.

4   From this research, we can understand the *religious meaning* of these *ancient Native American roads*.

| **Summarizing** |

In the reading passage, the purpose of *the ancient Native American roads* is discussed. There are two supporting arguments. The first is that roads were used *for transportation*. This is based on the fact that the roads were *very wide and straight*, meaning that they could have accommodated a large number of people. The second issue discussed is *the religious meaning* of the roads. According to the passage, *the shape and the location* of the roads were of great religious significance.

Script 02-05

**Professor:** Now, I want to address the debate in archaeological circles concerning the purpose of the ancient roads found throughout the U.S. In spite of their best efforts, archaeologists have not been able to reach any conclusions about them. The reason is that there is simply not enough evidence to determine what the roads were used for.

All right, so some archaeologists have put forth the idea that these roads were built solely for transportation. Well, the fact is that these roads were basically too large to have been used just to move people and things. Most of them are more than fifty yards wide, meaning that they were unnecessarily large to be used only for transportation. On top of that, there weren't any vehicles at that time. Back then, the only means of transportation available was walking. People rarely traveled more than a few miles from their homes during their lifetimes. This means that it was highly unlikely that the ancient Native Americans would have needed large, long highways to get around.

There's also the notion that the roads served religious purposes. Unfortunately, there is no evidence to support this. Do you have any idea why that is? Consider how the land has changed since these roads were first built. The majority of these ancient roads have been completely destroyed by centuries of farming and development, so it is impossible to determine the exact layout of these roads. And even if we could find the original roads, we still wouldn't be able to conclude that they were built for this reason. You see, many artifacts from these cultures have been lost, so we don't know what religion these people had or even if they were religious at all.

| Paraphrasing |

1   The roads could not have been used *only for transportation* because they were *much too big*.

2   Most people did not *travel far from their homes* over the course *of their lives*.

3   It is not possible to know *the original layout of these roads* due to all *the growth and the development* that has occurred over the years.

4   Because few *relics from these cultures* still exist, it is not possible to determine whether these people *even had religion*.

| Summarizing |

In the lecture, the professor explains that the purpose of the Native American roads remains unknown. His first argument is that the roads *were too large* to be used only for transportation. He adds that most people at that time *could only travel by foot* and rarely went far from their homes. His next point relates to *the religious meaning* of the roads. The instructor states that most of the roads have been destroyed over the years, so it is impossible to know *their original layouts*. Furthermore, he contends that there are not enough *artifacts from these societies* to know if they even had religion.

**Tandem Note-Taking**

p.94

Answers may vary.

| Reading | Listening |
|---|---|
| **Main Idea** | **Main Idea** |
| *Many compelling ideas have been put forth to explain the purpose of ancient roads.* | *There is not enough evidence to determine what these roads were used for.* |
| **First Supporting Argument** | **First Supporting Argument** |
| *One theory is that these roads were used for transportation.* | *The roads were too large to be used only for moving people and goods.* |
| Supporting Detail | Supporting Detail |
| *roads long, straight, wide* | *no vehicles; people did not travel far* |
| **Second Supporting Argument** | **Second Supporting Argument** |
| *The roads were of great religious significance.* | *There is no evidence to suggest that the roads had religious meaning.* |
| Supporting Detail | Supporting Detail |
| *shape and location of roads similar to constellation* | *roads destroyed over years; no artifacts* |

**Strong Response**

p.96

| Critical Analysis |

1   In the lecture, however, the professor contradicts these assumptions. / The instructor starts his lecture by expressing his doubts that the roads were used for transportation. / The professor goes on to question the theory that the roads were built for religious purposes.

2   He explains that because the roads were so wide, they could not have been used only for this purpose. / The professor adds that there were no vehicles at the time, so people were not able to travel very far anyway. / He explains that there is no evidence

to support this idea because the roads have been destroyed by many years of development. / He further states that few artifacts from these ancient cultures still exist, so archaeologists are not sure whether these ancient people even had any religious beliefs.

3   significance

4   It means to hold comfortably without crowding. The sentence that explains this is: His arguments refute the reading passage's assertion that these ancient roads were built to accommodate a large number of people traveling between villages.

5   The instructor starts her lecture by… / The professor adds… / The lecturer goes on to… / He further states…

**Weak Response**                                    p.97

| Critical Analysis |

1   ⓒ

Answer ⓒ is the best choice because it clearly explains the main idea from the reading passage. Answers Ⓐ and Ⓑ misrepresent this information.

2   ⓒ

Answer ⓒ is the best choice because this sentence gives additional information about the road mentioned in the sentence that comes before it.

3   The reading passage states that archaeologists understand the purpose of these ancient roads while the lecturer raises doubts about these claims. / Since the roads were very straight, they easily allowed people to travel between villages. / In the lecture, the professor argues that these ideas about the roads might not be correct.

▶ Chapter | 05 Independent Writing

**Meeting the Needs of Others to Be Happy**

**Generating Ideas**                                 p.98

**Idea Box**   **Agree**

1   *People like to improve other people's lives. They also like the way they feel after helping others.*

2   *They can spend time working at charities. They can also lend people money or other things they need.*

3   *People often feel happy after helping others in need. They may also feel satisfied.*

Reason 1: *People feel good when they can help others improve their lives.*

Reason 2: *It makes people happy when those they help show their appreciation.*

**Idea Box**   **Disagree**

1   They want to improve their lives and feel good at the same time.

2   *Some people are selfish and do not care about others. Other people would simply rather focus on their own lives.*

3   *It can solve a person's problems while also making the person feel better.*

Reason 1: *People can feel pleased with themselves when they take care of their own needs.*

Reason 2: *Many people are not interested in helping others who need assistance.*

**Planning**                                         p.99

Answers may vary.

| Agree | Disagree |
|---|---|
| **Thesis Statement** | **Thesis Statement** |
| *I think that people are definitely happier when they meet others' needs rather than their own.* | *I believe people become happier when they take care of themselves.* |
| **First Supporting Idea** | **First Supporting Idea** |
| *People feel good when they can help others improve their lives.* | *People can feel pleased with themselves when they take care of their own needs.* |
| Supporting Example | Supporting Example |
| *worked at a homeless shelter; had a good feeling when I took care of others* | *uncle bought a new car; looked very happy* |
| **Second Supporting Idea** | **Second Supporting Idea** |
| *It makes people happy when those they help show their appreciation.* | *Many people are not interested in helping others who need assistance.* |
| Supporting Example | Supporting Example |
| *friend needed help; helped her; expressed thanks, so I felt wonderful* | *school fundraiser; many people didn't want to donate anything* |

| Conclusion | Conclusion |
|---|---|
| *For these reasons, I support the idea that people are happier when they meet the needs of others rather than their own needs.* | *People are actually happier when they help themselves, not when they help others.* |

## Strong Response                    p.101

| Critical Analysis |

1   While some people become happier when they meet the needs of others rather than their own needs, I strongly disagree with this statement. / For starters, when people look after their own needs, they become very happy. / Furthermore, there are a large number of people who lack interest in taking care of other people's needs. / People are not happier when helping others rather than themselves.

2   For example, my uncle just bought a brand-new car a few days ago. / He drove his car to my family's house to show it to us yesterday. / He was so proud of his car and looked extremely happy as he was talking about it. / I could easily tell that he was happy after buying that car. / His previous car was old and broke down frequently. / So he took care of his own needs by acquiring a new vehicle. / I have never seen someone take care of another person's needs and look as happy as my uncle did yesterday. / Last month, my school had a fundraiser. / The school needed money to improve its facilities. / Many students visited local residents to tell them about the event. / I was one of those students. / Although a few people were willing to donate, the majority were not interested even in giving a small amount of money. / Some of them were actually quite rude about it.

3   the writer's uncle buying a new car for himself / people refusing to donate to a fundraiser

## Weak Response                    p.102

| Critical Analysis |

1   Ⓑ

    Answer Ⓑ is the best choice because it supports the main idea of the response. Answers Ⓐ and Ⓒ do not clearly support the central thesis.

2   Another reason I agree with the statement is that there are many unselfish people.

3   [Explain how some people volunteer their time to help others in need. Give examples such as

volunteering at homeless shelters or food banks.]

4   In fact, these people frequently prefer to assist others before they help themselves. / To begin with, there are many people who feel good when they help others with problems. / When my brother returned home, it was too late for him to study. / She does not worry about herself.

◗▶ Chapter | 06 Integrated Writing

Botany: **Preventing Mimosa Trees from Growing Too Much**

## Reading                    p.104

| Paraphrasing |

1   It is *an invasive species* because it can take over *the area where it grows*.

2   The mimosa *grows at a fast rate* and can *crowd out other plants*.

3   A gardener can *take seed pods off the tree* or pick them up after they *fall onto the ground*.

4   By *cutting deeply* enough into the tree, *its upper part* will die.

| Summarizing |

The mimosa tree is *an ornamental tree* that can take over people's yards. It is hard to *get rid of* once it starts growing. The mimosa tree *produces seed pods* that a person can take from a tree or pick up off the ground. That can keep trees from growing. A person can also *cut down trees* at the ground level or use girdling by *cutting off some bark*. Either method will make the trees die.

## Listening                    p.106

Script  02-06

**Professor:** This is a mimosa tree. It's rather beautiful, isn't it? The pink flowers are particularly attractive. Unfortunately, once mimosa trees start growing, they're almost impossible to get rid of. Some people have suggested ways to remove them, but these ideas have problems.

One suggestion I frequently hear is to collect the seeds. Well, mimosa trees produce thousands of seeds on a yearly basis. That's a lot of work you'll have to do to collect every seed. You're likely to miss many. You should also know that mimosa seeds can remain viable in the soil for several years and not grow if conditions aren't ideal. So you could have seeds from several years in the past suddenly germinate one year. And let's not forget about birds and other animals spreading seeds. You see, trying to get rid of the seeds is a monumental task.

It's possible to cut down mimosa trees and to use girdling to kill them. They are effective. But mimosa trees resprout. This means that if the roots remain in the ground, new trees can grow even after the original tree has died. Merely cutting the trees down near the soil isn't effective. You have to physically dig up the trees to remove the roots. That's possible, but it's a lot of hard work. Most people aren't willing to put in that much effort to remove mimosas, so the trees eventually take over their yards.

| **First Supporting Argument** | **First Supporting Argument** |
|---|---|
| *A person can prevent seed pods from getting into the soil.* | *It is nearly impossible to get rid of all the seeds from the tree.* |
| Supporting Detail | Supporting Detail |
| *take off the tree; pick up off the ground* | *thousands of seeds a year; can stay in the soil for years* |
| **Second Supporting Argument** | **Second Supporting Argument** |
| *A person can physically destroy the trees.* | *New trees can resprout from roots that are still in the ground.* |
| Supporting Detail | Supporting Detail |
| *cut trees down at ground level; use girdling by cutting off bark* | *need to dig up roots; new trees will grow; too much work for most people* |

## | Paraphrasing |

1   It is *nearly impossible* to get rid of mimosa trees in places where they are growing.

2   It is possible for mimosa seeds to *stay in the soil* for years without growing until *the time is right*.

3   Getting rid of the seeds is *extremely hard to do*.

4   As long as *there are still roots*, new trees can *grow from them* even if the original tree is gone.

## | Summarizing |

In the lecture, the professor points out that the suggested ways of *getting rid of mimosa trees* have problems. She mentions that mimosa trees produce *thousands of seeds each year*. Getting all of them will be hard. The seeds can also grow years after they have fallen into the soil and may also be *spread by animals*. The problem with cutting down the trees and girdling is that *the roots remain*. New trees can resprout from the roots. *Digging up the roots* is possible, but that is too much work for most people.

p.108

**Tandem Note-Taking**

Answers may vary.

| Reading | Listening |
|---|---|
| **Main Idea** | **Main Idea** |
| *It is possible to prevent mimosa trees from growing too much.* | *The suggested methods of getting rid of mimosa trees all have problems.* |

**Strong Response**     p.110

## | Critical Analysis |

1   However, the professor counters by stating that the suggested solutions all have problems. / In this way, the professor casts doubt on the solution in the reading passage that every seed can be collected to prevent new trees from growing. / She therefore goes against the argument in the reading passage that cutting down trees and using girdling can remove undesired mimosa trees.

2   The professor points out that mimosa trees grow thousands of seeds. / Collecting every seed would be difficult. / In addition, the seeds can germinate after several years of being in the ground and be spread by animals. / The professor also argues that mimosa trees can resprout from roots that remain in the ground. / She claims that the only way to get rid of them is to dig up the roots. / But this is too much work for most people.

3   collecting

4   It means to stop. The sentence that explains this is: In this way, the professor casts doubt on the solution in the reading passage that every seed can be removed to prevent new trees from growing.

5   However, the professor… / In addition, the seeds… / In this way, the professor… / The professor also argues that… / But this is too much…

| Critical Analysis |

1   Ⓐ

Answer Ⓐ is the best choice because it most clearly explains this argument from the reading passage. Answer Ⓑ misrepresents information in the passage while Answer Ⓒ contains information that is not mentioned in the passage.

2   Ⓑ

Answer Ⓑ is the best choice because this sentence mentions that it is too difficult for most people to dig up the roots.

3   The reading passage claims that it is possible to remove mimosa trees. / The professor says that there are many problems involved in removing mimosa trees. / So a person cannot pick up all of the seeds. / Next, the professor mentions that mimosa trees can grow again.

▶ Chapter | 06 Independent Writing

## Governments Should Focus on Health Care

**Generating Ideas**                                        p.112

**Idea Box** **Agree**

1   When more people are healthy, more work can be done, and more money can be spent.

2   Governments should do everything they can to make their people happy and healthy.

3   They are easier to fix in that people already know how to solve the problems.

**Reason 1:** Being healthy is the most important thing in a person's life.

**Reason 2:** Fixing the environment will take a long time.

**Idea Box** **Disagree**

1   Only some people need health care, but everybody has to live with the environment.

2   The environment can create health problems resulting from pollution.

3   They are easier to fix in that everyone can agree more easily about what needs to be done.

**Reason 1:** The environment affects everybody in the world.

**Reason 2:** Solving environmental issues can prevent other problems from occurring.

**Planning**                                                p.113

Answers may vary.

| Agree | Disagree |
|---|---|
| **Thesis Statement** <br><br> I contend that governments must make health care their most important issue. | **Thesis Statement** <br><br> While health care is important, I believe that nations must focus more on the environment. |
| **First Supporting Idea** <br><br> Being healthy is the most important thing in a person's life. | **First Supporting Idea** <br><br> The environment affects everybody in the world. |
| Supporting Example <br><br> cannot do anything without health | Supporting Example <br><br> water running out because of pollution |
| **Second Supporting Idea** <br><br> Fixing the environment will take a long time. | **Second Supporting Idea** <br><br> Solving environmental issues can prevent other problems from occurring. |
| Supporting Example <br><br> fix health care first and environment later | Supporting Example <br><br> health problems from pollution |
| **Conclusion** <br><br> In conclusion, I feel that health care is a more pressing issue than the environment. | **Conclusion** <br><br> I believe that governments should make environmental issues their top priority. |

**Strong Response**                                         p.115

| Critical Analysis |

1   Therefore, it is clear that governments around the world need to make environmental issues their top priority. / The environment is the one thing that affects everyone in the world. / On top of this, addressing environmental issues can help solve other problems and prevent them from occurring in the future. / Although governments around the world have many serious issues to tackle, I believe that they should make environmental issues their top priority.

2   For example, consider the main resource that we all take for granted: water. / Clean water supplies all over the world are running out. / This is happening for a variety of reasons. / They include pollution by companies and overuse by individuals. / As serious

as the water problem is, it can still be corrected but only if governments make an effort to do so. / Think about how the environment can affect a person's health. / In developing nations such as China, the air is polluted due to smog from factories and automobiles. / As a result of this pollution, thousands of people develop health problems and have to go to the hospital each year. / Virtually all of these cases could be prevented if the Chinese government made stricter regulations concerning air pollution.

3   water supplies running low as a result of pollution / pollution creates health problems

**Weak Response**                                    p.116

| Critical Analysis |

1   Ⓒ

Answer Ⓒ is the best choice because it gives an example to support the argument in the third body paragraph. Answer Ⓐ goes against the main idea of the response, and Answer Ⓑ does not directly support it.

2   Furthermore, most people cannot afford to pay for their own health care.

3   [Give an example of a sick person who cannot work. Describe the problems that can occur to this person's family as a result.]

4   Although many people worry about the environment, I believe that health care is a greater concern for governments around the world. / Because health care is so expensive, most people need the government to help them pay for it. / It would be less expensive for the government to fix healthcare issues than it would be for it to address the problems of the environment. / While environmental issues are of great concern, they are not as important as improving health care.

▶ Chapter | 07 Integrated Writing

Business: **Paying Employees on Commission**

**Reading**                                          p.118

| Paraphrasing |

1   When paid for the amount of work *they complete*, employees tend to work *more quickly and effectively*.

2   Employees paid on commission finish their tasks *almost one-third faster* compared to employees *paid flat salaries*.

3   Workers paid on commission can earn *two or three times* their original salaries.

4   People who are paid for the amount of work they do are *happier with their jobs* since their *diligence pays off*.

| Summarizing |

The author of the reading passage contends that *paying employees on commission* benefits both *employers and employees*. It benefits employers in that workers become *more productive*. On top of this, employees paid on commission do work of *a better quality*. At the same time, receiving a commission is good for employees because they are able to *earn more money*. Not only does this allow them to enjoy a higher quality of life, but it also gives workers *greater job satisfaction*.

**Listening**                                        p.120

Script 02-07

**Professor:** We all know that everybody would like to make more money. So it seems that paying employees on commission is a great idea. Well, I believe that foregoing steady salaries in favor of a commission may not be for everyone. Still skeptical? Okay, then listen to this.

Of course, some jobs are well suited to commission-based payments. Most sales jobs, for example, pay on straight commission. Other jobs, however, cannot or should not be paid in this way. A good example of this would be teachers. Allow me to elaborate. Let's assume that teachers are paid based on the number of students who pass their classes. What do you think would happen in this case? That's right. Every student would always pass every class. The teachers might benefit from this situation, but would the students? To me, it doesn't seem so.

Here's another point. Being paid on commission does not always guarantee an increase in salary. Sure, some people do very well, but most people's incomes can fluctuate greatly from month to month. What I mean is that during some months, they can make a lot of money, but during other months, they can make virtually none. Let's consider a person who works in advertising. In a month when that person lands a big contract, she can earn a lot of money. In other months, when she doesn't get any contracts, she might not make anything. This lack of stability can cause employees to feel uncomfortable with their financial situations, and this can greatly reduce their work productivity.

| Paraphrasing |

1   There are certain *types of positions* that should be *paid on commission*.

2   No students would ever fail *any of their classes*.

3   Workers who are paid for the number of *tasks they complete* do not always *earn more money*.

4   People who do not have *steady salaries* can become nervous about *their incomes*, which makes them unable to *work efficiently*.

| Summarizing |

The instructor opposes paying *all employees on commission*. He gives two arguments in favor of his opinion. First, the professor explains that not all jobs should be paid on commission. To illustrate this, he uses the example of teachers. He says that teachers would benefit from *commission-based salaries*, but students would not. Next, the lecturer talks about how being paid for the amount of work done does not always *guarantee an increase* in salary. He clarifies this by talking about how *the amount of money* a person earns *can fluctuate greatly* from month to month.

**Tandem Note-Taking**                                    p.122

Answers may vary.

| Reading | Listening |
|---|---|
| **Main Idea** | **Main Idea** |
| *Paying employees on commission benefits both employers and employees.* | *Not all employees should be paid on commission.* |
| **First Supporting Argument** | **First Supporting Argument** |
| *Offering employees commission-based payments makes them work more efficiently.* | *Some jobs cannot or should not be paid on commission.* |
| Supporting Detail | Supporting Detail |
| *do work 30% faster; better quality* | *teachers; education quality go down* |
| **Second Supporting Argument** | **Second Supporting Argument** |
| *Employees who work on commission can earn more money.* | *Being paid on commission does not always guarantee a higher salary.* |

| Supporting Detail | Supporting Detail |
|---|---|
| *double, triple salary; more work satisfaction* | *income fluctuates; become uncomfortable* |

**Strong Response**                                       p.124

| Critical Analysis |

1   The professor, however, asserts that paying on commission might not benefit all workers. / The lecturer begins by stating that not all jobs should be paid on commission. / The professor also believes that employees paid on commission do not always make more money.

2   He gives the example of teachers. / He argues that teachers should not be paid on commission because the quality of education would decrease substantially. / He says that the amount of money an employee on commission earns can fluctuate greatly each month. / In some months, they can make a lot of money. / In other months, they might make none at all. / This often makes people uncomfortable about their financial situations.

3   flat

4   It means to keep changing to a large degree. The sentence that explains this is: He says that the amount of money an employee on commission earns can fluctuate greatly each month.

5   The lecturer begins by stating… / The professor goes on to state that … / On the other hand…

**Weak Response**                                         p.125

| Critical Analysis |

1   (A)

Answer (A) is the best choice because it most accurately expresses the idea of the highlighted sentence. Answer (B) is too general while Answer (C) misrepresents the information in the sentence.

2   (B)

Answer (B) is the best choice because this sentence gives additional information about why teachers should not be paid on commission, which is the argument presented in the first body paragraph.

3   The lecturer's argument casts doubt on the claims made in the reading passage. / This contrasts the reading passage's assertion that workers paid on commission complete their work more quickly and effectively. / Next, the professor questions the argument that commission-based salaries result in

higher incomes for employees.

Chapter | 07 Independent Writing

## Working at a High-Paying Job with Low Security

### Generating Ideas
p.126

**Idea Box** **High-Paying Job**

1  *By earning more money, a person does not have to worry about paying bills or buying food.*

2  *Changing jobs can often make a person's life more interesting because that person can work at many different places.*

3  *With a high salary, a person can afford a comfortable home, nice clothing, and good food.*

**Reason 1:** *The amount of money a person earns directly affects that person's quality of life.*

**Reason 2:** *Finding another job is not difficult.*

**Idea Box** **Secure Job**

1  *Having a secure job makes it possible to plan for the future, which money alone cannot do.*

2  *A person could never become completely settled and would have to worry about the future.*

3  *No, having a lot of money does not matter as long as people can live comfortably without stress.*

**Reason 1:** *Job security is more important than earning a high income.*

**Reason 2:** *Earning a lot of money is not necessary.*

### Planning
p.127

Answers may vary.

| High-Paying Job | Secure Job |
|---|---|
| **Thesis Statement** | **Thesis Statement** |
| *I would prefer to work at a high-paying job with little job security.* | *I would rather have a secure job even if it did not pay a lot of money.* |
| **First Supporting Idea** | **First Supporting Idea** |
| *The amount of money a person earns directly affects that person's quality of life.* | *Job security is more important than earning a high income.* |
| **Supporting Example** | **Supporting Example** |
| *brother makes a lot of money; lives well* | *buy a house; plan for the future* |
| **Second Supporting Idea** | **Second Supporting Idea** |
| *Finding another job is not difficult.* | *Earning a lot of money is not necessary.* |
| **Supporting Example** | **Supporting Example** |
| *friend found new jobs; better pay* | *have enough with a modest income* |
| **Conclusion** | **Conclusion** |
| *Higher-paying jobs with less job security are the way to go.* | *Living a comfortable and stable life is very important, so having a stable but low-paying job is better.* |

### Strong Response
p.129

| Critical Analysis |

1  It is for this reason that I would prefer to work at a higher-paying job that offers less job security. / For one, the amount of money a person earns directly affects that person's quality of life. / In addition, finding another job is not difficult. / However, for people like me who enjoy earning a lot of money and do not mind changing jobs every few years, higher-paying jobs with less job security are the way to go.

2  He works as a manager at a major company and earns a very large paycheck. / As a result, he is able to afford many nice things for himself. / For instance, he lives in a large apartment in a wealthy part of the city, drives a luxury car, and wears only the best clothing. / Although some people may think these sorts of things are unnecessary, they allow him to live a better life. / This, in turn, positively affects his health and happiness. / Not long ago, she graduated from college with a degree in engineering. / She was quickly able to get a job with a starting salary of 50,000 dollars per year. / She worked at that job for six months until she was suddenly fired one day. / Within a month, my friend was able to find a similar position with even better pay. / Since then, she has worked at four different jobs, each one with better pay and benefits.

3  older brother's situation as a highly paid manager / friend who lost her job but found other quickly

| Critical Analysis |

1   (B)

Answer (B) is the best choice because it gives an example to support the argument in the second body paragraph why earning a lot of money is not necessary.

2   On top of this, earning a high salary is not that important.

3   [Explain how a relative with a steady job is happier than a relative who has to change jobs constantly.]

4   Some people might prefer working at a high-paying job, but I think that a lower-paying secure job is superior. / People who stay at the same job for many years have more comfortable and steady lives than those who change jobs frequently. / Living a comfortable and stable life is very important, so having a stable but low-paying job is better.

Chapter | 08 Integrated Writing

Communication: **Interactive Voice Response Technology**

**Reading**

p.132

| Paraphrasing |

1   IVR systems will present callers *with questions* to determine *the type of assistance* they require.

2   With IVR systems, callers do not have to *wait to speak to a staff member* when they phone a call center.

3   These systems are *unquestionably better* when callers would rather not *speak with another person*.

4   Callers tend not to give their *honest opinions* when talking to *a live representative*.

| Summarizing |

In the reading passage, the writer asserts that *IVR technology is required* in modern telecommunications. The author's first argument is that IVR systems make call center services more efficient. This is illustrated by the fact that these systems *can sort callers* and connect them to *appropriate representatives* more quickly. The writer's next argument is that IVR technology allows information to be exchanged *more accurately*. The reason is that callers are more honest when dealing with one of these systems.

**Listening**

p.134

Script 02-08

**Professor:** If there is one piece of technology that I completely despise, it is interactive voice response systems. These systems are used by customer call centers everywhere to make their services more efficient. But rather than improving customer service, these systems actually hinder it.

First of all, IVR systems do not actually save time. Why do you think that is? Well, think about how these systems work. In order to find the information you need, you have to listen to a series of menus and press a button to make your selection. Sometimes these menus are not organized well, so it can be difficult to determine which button you need to press. And if you press the wrong button, you have to go back to the previous menu and start over again. This just wastes time. Simply put, it is much easier to get an answer from a person than to try to navigate a series of confusing prerecorded menus.

What's more is that interactive voice systems are too impersonal. Generally, most people want their questions answered by another human being. For instance, how does it make you feel when you call your bank and deal only with a prerecorded voice message? Unimportant? Insignificant? You're not alone. Most customers feel this way. This is why some companies are actually switching back to staffed call centers. They know that customer satisfaction is more important than saving a bit of money with these IVR systems.

| Paraphrasing |

1   Not only do IVR systems fail to *improve customer service*, but they actually *make it worse*.

2   The menus in IVR are not always *logically organized*, which makes it *hard to find* the information you need.

3   It is simpler to get information *from another person* than to search through *a series of complex menus*.

4   Companies understand that *cutting costs with IVR systems* is not as important as *keeping customers happy*.

| Summarizing |

In his lecture, the instructor *criticizes IVR systems* because they worsen customer service. He supports his opinion with two main ideas. The first is that IVR technology *does not save time*. This is due to the fact that callers have to navigate *a series of menus* that are sometimes not organized very well. He also dislikes IVR systems for being *too impersonal*. He says that most people would rather speak to another person, and it is for this reason that many companies are now *switching back to staffed* call centers.

**Tandem Note-Taking**                                    p.136

Answers may vary.

| Reading | Listening |
|---|---|
| **Main Idea** | **Main Idea** |
| *Modern telecommunications would not be possible without IVR systems.* | *IVR systems do not improve customer service but actually worsen it.* |
| **First Supporting Argument** | **First Supporting Argument** |
| *IVR systems allow companies to make their services more efficient.* | *This technology does not save time.* |
| Supporting Detail | Supporting Detail |
| *screen and sort callers; get immediate info* | *difficult to use menus* |
| **Second Supporting Argument** | **Second Supporting Argument** |
| *These systems allow callers to remain anonymous, which allows information to be exchanged accurately.* | *IVR systems are too impersonal.* |
| Supporting Detail | Supporting Detail |
| *callers more honest; better for privacy* | *rather talk to person* |

**Strong Response**                                       p.138

| Critical Analysis |

1 The reading passage presents arguments strongly in favor of this technology, but the lecturer questions the validity of these arguments. / First, the reading passage claims that IVR systems help callers save time because they help call centers provide personalized service for each caller. / Then, to refute the reading passage's assertion that the anonymity of IVR systems is a benefit, the instructor criticizes IVR systems for being too impersonal.

2 He states that IVR systems do not make telecommunication services more efficient because they require callers to waste time navigating menus to find the information they seek. / He goes on to say that most callers would feel more comfortable talking to an actual person. / He says these systems can make callers feel unimportant and insignificant.

/ The professor explains that many call centers are now switching back to human representatives because of this.

3 anonymity

4 It means not important. The sentence that explains this is: He says these systems can make callers feel unimportant and insignificant.

5 First… / He goes on to say … / Then…

**Weak Response**                                         p.139

| Critical Analysis |

1 ⓒ

Answer ⓒ is the best choice because it more accurately summarizes the lecturer's argument. Answers Ⓐ and Ⓑ misrepresent the information in the lecture.

2 ⓒ

Answer ⓒ is the best choice because this sentence gives additional information about why IVR systems are confusing to use, which is the argument made in the previous sentence.

3 In the reading passage, it is argued that IVR systems are needed in modern telecommunications. / First, the reading passage states that IVR systems let companies offer more efficient service. / Next, the passage argues that this technology allows callers to exchange information more accurately. / The lecturer contradicts this argument.

◗ Chapter | **08 Independent Writing**

**A Person Working in a Group Must Accept Criticism**

**Generating Ideas**                                      p.140

**Idea Box**   **Agree**

1 *The purpose is to generate many ideas from different people and to use the best ideas.*

2 *It would become more difficult to finish on time because the members will not work as quickly.*

3 *This person can lower the overall quality of the material produced by the group.*

**Reason 1:** *All members of a group must work together to complete their task.*

**Reason 2:** *A person who cannot accept criticism will lower the quality of the group's work.*

Idea Box **Disagree**

1   *A group can save time because its members will not spend time arguing over ideas.*

2   *The person may know that his or her ideas are better than those of the other group members.*

3   *It can make it easier for other members to focus on their tasks and not worry about the stubborn member.*

**Reason 1:** *Criticizing the ideas of your group members can waste valuable time.*

**Reason 2:** *People may not listen to criticism if they know their ideas are better.*

## Planning p.141

Answers may vary.

| Agree | Disagree |
|---|---|
| **Thesis Statement** | **Thesis Statement** |
| *I entirely agree that a person cannot work successfully in a group if that individual cannot accept criticism.* | *I contend that a person can contribute to a group successfully even if that individual cannot accept criticism.* |
| **First Supporting Idea** | **First Supporting Idea** |
| *All members of a group must work together to complete their task.* | *Criticizing the ideas of your group members can waste valuable time.* |
| Supporting Example | Supporting Example |
| *stubborn member; not able to finish project* | *spent whole time arguing; did not finish* |
| **Second Supporting Idea** | **Second Supporting Idea** |
| *A person who cannot accept criticism will lower the quality of the group's work.* | *People may not listen to criticism if they know their ideas are better.* |
| Supporting Example | Supporting Example |
| *literature class presentation; got B instead of A* | *experienced person; no need to listen to others* |
| **Conclusion** | **Conclusion** |
| *Overall, I believe that in order to be successful in a group, a person must be willing to accept criticism.* | *People who do not listen to criticism can still be successful in a group.* |

**Strong Response** p.143

| **Critical Analysis** |

1   I entirely agree with the statement that a person cannot work successfully in a group if that individual cannot accept criticism. / When working in a group, it is important that all members work together to complete their task. / Furthermore, a person who cannot accept criticism will lower the quality of the work produced by the entire group. / Overall, I believe that in order to be successful in a group, a person must be willing to accept criticism.

2   There was one member of my group who would not listen to our suggestions about how to improve her ideas. / She would often become angry if we did not completely agree with her. / Eventually, she refused to do any more work for the group. / As a result, the rest of us had to do our work and hers, so we were not able to finish our assignment on time. / One member of my group refused to let any of us edit his speech, which contained several mistakes. / When our group finally gave our presentation, most of us did well, except for the stubborn member. / In the end, our group got a B for our presentation. / Had the one member listened to our suggestions, we might have gotten an A.

3   not completing a group project in high school / getting a worse grade on a project for literature class

**Weak Response** p.144

| **Critical Analysis** |

1   Ⓐ

Answer Ⓐ is the best choice because it clearly explains why the author's brother did not listen to the criticism offered by his group members. Answer Ⓑ contradicts the main idea of the response while Answer Ⓒ does not clearly support it.

2   People may also not listen to criticism if they know their ideas are better.

3   [Explain what the brother's ideas were and why they were better than those of his partners.]

4   Some people believe that working in a group means having to accept criticism, but this is not always the case. / First, criticizing the ideas of your group members can waste valuable time. / Once, when I worked in a group, there was a member who would not listen to the criticism of others.

Task 1

### Listening

**Script** 03-03

**Professor:** These days, there are so many ways that scientists want to change our food. They love to report the positive aspects of their experiments, but they rarely report the bad. Take food irradiation, for example. Although some would like us to believe otherwise, this process has some serious drawbacks that must be noted.

Supporters of irradiation say this kills harmful organisms in the food. Sure, it kills them—most of them. But what happens to the ones that are not killed? Ah, here is the danger. These organisms cannot be killed by irradiation. They are the stronger insects or bacteria. Then what happens? They reproduce and create more of these strong organisms. Over time, irradiation will create super bugs that cannot easily be killed.

Fans of food irradiation will also say that it preserves the vitamins in food. Well, that's not always the case. Many studies have shown that irradiation breaks down vitamin C compounds in foods. Vitamin C is an extremely important nutrient for humans. Other vitamins and minerals are damaged as well. In fact, irradiated food can lose five to eighty percent of its nutrients. At some point, we have to ask the following question: Do we want fresh food that has no nutritional value?

Speaking of fresh food, I'd like to address another false belief about irradiated food. Supporters of this method will tell you that irradiation keeps food perfectly fresh. Well, not so fast. Fruits and vegetables are usually irradiated before they become fully ripe. But food tastes best when it is perfectly ripe, doesn't it? Sure, the food may last a long time, but if it tastes bad, who wants to eat it? The reality is that food irradiation is an interesting idea, but it simply has too many problems.

### • Model Answer •

The reading passage argues that irradiation is an excellent way to preserve food. The lecturer disputes the reading passage by arguing that food irradiation causes more harm than good.

The first supporting argument offered by the reading focuses on destroying pests. Irradiation kills insects and organisms that live on the food. Doing this makes them safer to eat and protects food supplies. The professor counters by pointing out that the strong organisms will survive irradiation and reproduce. They will create super bugs that cannot easily be killed.

The reading continues by stating the health benefits of food irradiation. Unlike other methods, irradiation stops the food's aging process and preserves its vitamins and nutrients. The professor claims that this assertion is untrue. She says that vitamins are actually destroyed and mentions vitamin C as an example. According to the professor, irradiated food can lose up to eighty percent of its nutritional value.

As a final supporting argument, the passage highlights the benefits of the long-lasting freshness of irradiated food. It uses the example of a banana, which ordinarily goes bad after about a week. After irradiation, it may last for months, thereby reducing waste by giving people more time to consume it. The professor questions the value of this freshness. She says that food is usually irradiated before it ripens. Therefore, although the food may last much longer, its quality is greatly diminished.

Task 2

### • Model Answer •

I agree with the statement. I strongly believe that the government needs to increase the price of electricity in order to encourage people to conserve it. Let me explain three reasons why I support the government doing this.

The first reason is that too many people waste electricity these days. For instance, people constantly leave the lights on in rooms after they go out. They also leave their television sets and computers on when they leave their homes. My brother and sister always do this even when my parents remind them not to. Not turning off appliances is a huge waste of electricity. People should be punished for doing that. One form of punishment is having to pay higher prices for electricity.

In addition, most electricity is created by burning fossil fuels such as coal, oil, and gas. These are nonrenewable resources, so there is a limited supply of them on the Earth. For that reason, we should not waste these valuable resources. If people have to pay higher prices for electricity, they will try to use less of it. By doing that, they will conserve our natural resources.

Finally, nowadays, lots of people are purchasing electric vehicles because they think that those cars are good for the environment. But those vehicles still need electricity to run. If the price of electricity is higher, then people might decide not to drive electric cars. Instead, they might use public transportation. That will be better for the environment. It will also help decrease traffic on the roads, especially in big cities. So people will be able to arrive at their jobs and homes much more quickly each morning and evening.

There are clearly several advantages to the government raising the price of electricity. People will stop wasting electricity, they will conserve natural resources, and they will stop driving electric cars and instead take public transportation. To me, it is clear that the government should act now and raise the price of electricity.

## Actual Test 02 p.156

### Task 1

### Listening

**Script** 03-07

**Professor:** These days, many people are discussing building high-speed trains. They claim that high-speed trains offer plenty of advantages. Well, these people couldn't be more wrong. There's no need to waste time or money on high-speed trains.

Now, it's true that high-speed trains can move fast. But the problem is they don't go where people want them to. By that, I mean the stations serviced by high-speed trains are in inconvenient locations. So when people get off the trains, they aren't close to their workplaces or homes. As a result, they have to take some other form of transportation to reach their final destinations. Because high-speed trains are so inconvenient, not enough people are willing to take them.

I often hear people claim that high-speed trains will reduce the need for expensive road maintenance. But consider that road construction methods are improving every year. There are even self-healing asphalt and concrete nowadays. If cities use these advanced construction materials, expensive road maintenance won't be necessary. Roads built with self-healing asphalt have lifespans of between forty and eighty years. Because the streets themselves can fix most problems, road maintenance costs can be eliminated.

As a final point, let's think about the prices of high-speed trains. Yes, it's true that they are fairly fuel efficient. So they save money in that regard.

However, the cost of building a high-speed train is astronomical. In the northeast part of the United States, Amtrak, an American railway operator, estimates it could build 1.6 kilometers of high-speed rail for half a billion dollars. That's simply ridiculous. We're talking billions of dollars to make a single railway line.

High-speed trains should be avoided. They have few advantages, and their disadvantages are enormous. Instead, governments should focus on other methods of transportation.

#### • Model Answer •

The lecture and the reading passage are about high-speed trains. The lecturer challenges the claims made in the reading passage that high-speed trains have many advantages.

The lecturer begins by pointing out that the stations visited by high-speed trains are inconveniently located. So people must take other forms of transportation to reach their destinations. This makes few people want to take high-speed trains. The professor's argument goes against the one in the reading passage. It argues that the fast speeds of the trains will make people want to take them.

Second, the lecturer points out that roads can be made with self-healing asphalt and concrete. These will eliminate the need for expensive road construction. So the lecturer refutes the argument in the reading passage that high-speed trains will reduce the need for expensive road maintenance.

The lecturer's final point is about the cost of constructing high-speed trains. He argues that building a single railway line will cost billions of dollars. For example, he mentions that Amtrak thinks it can build 1.6 kilometers of high-speed railway for half a billion dollars. This challenges the claim in the reading passage that the fuel efficiency of high-speed trains makes them cheap options.

The professor successfully points out several disadvantages of high-speed trains. His arguments show that countries should avoid building them since high-speed trains have few benefits.

### Task 2

#### • Model Answer •

The role of a teacher is primarily to give knowledge to students. Some educators, however, believe that teachers should also promote the self-confidence of students. While this notion may at first seem unusual, I believe there are actually some critical benefits of such a goal.

Self-confidence is a key aspect of learning. To use myself as an example, when I began studying English, everyone in my class was a beginner. As time went by, some of us showed faster improvement than others. I noticed that students who improved quickly had self-confidence. They were not afraid to make mistakes. As the adage says, "Practice makes perfect." The students who did not have self-confidence did not get as much practice. This was clear by their slower rates of learning.

In my experience, self-confidence also affects one's motivation to learn. When I was younger, I became interested in art. At first, I was truly terrible. I knew that my drawings were bad, but my first art teacher always praised them. She said I would become the next Leonardo da Vinci. My motivation increased, and I frequently practiced drawing in my free time. Later, I had an art teacher who always criticized the class. I found that my motivation was seriously damaged, and, eventually, I gave up learning art altogether. In the end, the teacher did not succeed in teaching me art because he ruined my motivation.

Finally, self-confidence can affect the rest of a student's life. We can see examples of people who had the self-confidence to take risks and succeed. Microsoft founder Bill Gates dropped out of Harvard University in order to start his career. It was a dangerous move, but he had the self-confidence to try it. Now, he is among the wealthiest people in the world. Without self-confidence, students may never find true success.

Consequently, teachers should emphasize building their students' self-confidence. Not only will it help the students succeed in their learning, but it will also prepare them to succeed in their adult lives.

# TOEFL®
## MAP
New
TOEFL®
Edition

### Writing

Intermediate